Helping Teens and Young Adults with Anxi

Helping Teens and Young Adults with Anxiety provides a unique structure for a complete ten-week programme, equipping secondary school, college, and university staff with the tools to support students who are experiencing anxiety.

Following on from the authors' best seller *Supporting Children and Young People with Anxiety*, this companion resource is tailored to meet the complex needs of teenagers and young people and provides a programme which can be run entirely independently. The intervention draws on a range of theoretical backgrounds and practical models of working and reflects recent improved understanding of the neuropsychology of stress and anxiety and an understanding of the effect that trauma can have on the body and mind. Presuming no prior experience on the part of the reader, the authors acknowledge the challenges involved in recognising anxiety and delivering tailored treatment and emphasise the roles of prevention and early intervention. All resources are photocopiable and downloadable and can be easily customised for use with children and parents.

Helping Teens and Young Adults with Anxiety provides an eclectic approach to managing anxiety and serves as an important text for education professionals working with young people in both academic and non-academic sectors.

Elizabeth Herrick and **Barbara Redman-White** are both educational psychologists. Their previous book, *Supporting Children and Young People with Anxiety: A Practical Guide*, was published by Routledge (2019).

Helen Hudson spent over twenty years working in the education sector and currently works for the NHS in their adult mental health programme.

Helping Teens and Young Adults with Anxiety

A Ten Session Programme

By Elizabeth Herrick, Barbara Redman-White, and Helen Hudson

Routledge
Taylor & Francis Group

LONDON AND NEW YORK

Cover images: © Dani Pasteau

First published 2023
by Routledge
4 Park Square, Milton Park, Abingdon, Oxon OX14 4RN

and by Routledge
605 Third Avenue, New York, NY 10158

Routledge is an imprint of the Taylor & Francis Group, an informa business

British Library Cataloguing-in-Publication Data
A catalogue record for this book is available from the British Library

Library of Congress Cataloging-in-Publication Data
A catalogue record has been requested for this book

ISBN: 978-1-032-01823-2 (hbk)
ISBN: 978-1-032-01839-3 (pbk)
ISBN: 978-1-003-18036-4 (ebk)

DOI: 10.4324/9781003180364

Typeset in Bembo
by Apex CoVantage, LLC

Access the Support Material: www.routledge.com/9781032018393

Contents

Introduction

This workbook was inspired by the highly positive response to our initial publication **Supporting Children and Young People with Anxiety** (2019). This publication provides a detailed practical guide to understanding and managing anxiety. The inclusion of a ten-session practical intervention to support small groups of children in managing their anxiety has been well received and widely used in schools. The intervention was used and evaluated in several different school settings, with the support of the University of Southampton. Findings have been very positive (Hadwin, Herrick, Redman-White, Supporting Children and Young People with Anxiety: A Pilot Study, presented at British Psychological Society Division of Child and Educational Psychologists Annual Conference, January 2020).

Further practical work, as well as developments in the psychological understanding of anxiety, led the authors to develop the content of the intervention further. Feedback from practitioners suggested that a practical workbook, designed specifically for working with older teenagers and young adults, would be a welcome addition to the original publication.

Recent developments including the coronavirus pandemic, economic turbulence, armed combat in Europe, and climate change have increased the anxiety for young people who are having to manage the pressure of deciding the best future path for their education and skills development. The current societal changes have led to increased uncertainty, fear, and insecurity about what the future holds.

However, we know as psychologists that there are effective ways to improve well-being for young people, provided there are the resources to deliver them. Educational settings will play a key role in helping promote young people's happiness and well-being during these unsettled times. We hope that schools, colleges, and universities will find this an easy-to-use programme as it is semi-scripted and has all the resources ready to print or photocopy. Equally, psychologists, social workers, counsellors, and others who typically provide emotional and mental health support to teens and young adults should benefit from the structured and wide-ranging approaches to supporting young people with anxiety.

Access the Support Material: www.routledge.com/9781032018393

How to Use This Book

The Intervention

All the resources in this book can be easily photocopied and are available as e-resources. The programme provided in this workbook involves directed approaches, with specific issues covered in each session. Each of the ten sessions addresses a different aspect of anxiety management. In our experience, students have strong but varied preferences for the types of approaches that appeal to them. In this programme, they are encouraged to try a range of methods and then adopt into their lifestyle those which are effective for them. Each session aims to teach a skill in a variety of ways: through direct explanation, discussion, exercises, video clips, and between-session practice tasks. There are facilitator's notes, a semi-scripted plan, and handouts for each session. Our aim is to make this an easy-to-use guide for professionals to be able to take off the shelf and use with a range of students. In the session plans following, the suggested script is in italics.

The gold standard for running this course would be to run all aspects of each session in around 45 minutes on a weekly basis, with all students completing tasks in between. Time between sessions is important to encourage consolidation of learning and practising new skills. However, as practitioners, we are aware of the many logistical issues of arranging a programme, especially in an educational setting. If it is not possible to match these arrangements, students will still benefit from completing parts of the course.

The authors have found that groups develop their own "personality" and will respond better to some teaching methods than others. A post-lockdown group recently made it clear that they had had enough of screens, much preferring activities and discussion, so we used the video clips sparingly. As the ideas are presented in an assortment of ways, the facilitator may choose to emphasise and spend more time on the activities preferred by each group. Equally, if a video clip is unavailable or unsuited to a particular group, the facilitator can choose an alternative with the same learning points or dispense with the video altogether for that session.

Educational settings might find that running the programme early in the academic year is beneficial as it allows for further consolidation and follow-up sessions over the rest of the year, though this is not essential. The group approach allows young people to learn from each other and recognise that they are not the only ones feeling the way they do.

Setting Up the Group

The authors would recommend a group size of around six young people, though the program has been run with both larger and smaller groups. Counsellors, social workers, and psychologists may have a clear set of clients suitable for such group work and choose to bring them together.

In an educational setting, there are several ways to select suitable young people. They may be referred for support by staff who know them well, they may self-refer, parents may have expressed concern, or there can be more general screening for specific year groups. Screening can reveal anxious students who might otherwise be "hidden" in a classroom setting, and their concerns may not be obvious to others. There are many free screeners available online, e.g., Strengths and Difficulties (Goodman et al., 2003), Core 10, GAD 7 (ages 11–17 and age 18+), RCADS (see references following). If young people are already receiving support from other mental health agencies, facilitators are advised to liaise with that provider to avoid overload for the individual and/or confusion from differences in the approaches employed.

Initial Planning

Once participants have been identified, it is important to gain informed consent both from them and preferably, if they are under 18 years of age, from their parents. Some schools take the view that specific parental consent is not needed if the course takes place during school time. If this is the case, then it is good practice to ensure that parents are fully informed. If the course is to take place outside a student's typical timetable, transport arrangements may need to be made, for which younger students may need parental assistance.

Young people should feel able to opt in or opt out of the group, depending on their motivation to complete the intervention and their willingness to work in a group. No young person should be expected to complete the programme if they are not comfortable doing so. We would recommend when selecting the group members that social relationships are considered. Some facilitators have suggested that it helps if each person in the group knows at least one other, although young people who have a very close friendship bond or are siblings may find it difficult to respond independently.

A suitable venue will be relatively private and quiet and will not be disturbed during the session. Where possible, it is beneficial to keep to the same venue for each session. Access to appropriate resources will be important, including internet access, flipchart/screen, tables, pens, pencils, and water. Depending on the time of day and what the students have done previously, the availability of drinks and snacks may assist students' attention and create a more relaxed atmosphere.

The group can be run by one facilitator, though there are advantages in having two. The presence of two facilitators provides a higher level of safety and security for both themselves and the participants. It enables discussion between sessions to ensure effective strategies are in place. It can also be a training opportunity for a staff member less familiar with this type of work to assist an experienced facilitator. However, the authors are aware that professionals are often working under resource constraints. If there is no co-facilitator, it would be helpful for the facilitator to identify a support system for themselves at this stage, in order that each session can be discussed and any changes to the approach agreed in line with the individual needs of the group members.

It may be helpful to run an initial planning meeting prior to the beginning of the intervention to explain the process to students, staff, and parents as appropriate. This would also be a suitable point to make transport arrangements for students who need assistance.

Confidentiality

When working with individuals, it is essential to be clear about confidentiality at the beginning. Facilitators should not offer confidentiality beyond the bounds that they can keep. A good guideline is to explain to young people that their personal contribution in the sessions remains confidential unless:

> "the client gives permission for information to be shared and/or the client reveals something which could be endangering themselves or others."

> Herrick and Redman-White, 2019

In the first session, ground rules for the group will be set jointly, which may include keeping what happens in the sessions to each other. However, it is not always easy or practical for young people to keep to confidentiality guidelines, so it is important to stress that each participant is responsible for how much and what they share in the group.

Evaluation

For young people to think about what they would like to achieve by attending the group, it is helpful to ask each student to set personal goals. A handout for this is given in Session 1. Students will be asked to keep this to refer to again in Session 10. As not all students are well organised, the facilitator may wish to keep copies of all the students' completed personal goals for any student who arrives at Session 10 without theirs. This provides a personalised evaluation for each student. Students are also asked to provide their evaluation of the course for the facilitator. A proforma for this is provided as a handout for Session 10.

When deciding on evaluation methods, there will necessarily be a balance between the level of detail provided and the ease of administration. If a formal, standardised evaluation is required, a screening tool such as the Strengths and Difficulties questionnaire could double as the baseline assessment and be repeated at the end of the ten-session intervention to track progress. This minimises the paperwork and analysis. However, it may be less subtle to small individual changes than other assessment tools, e.g., YP-CORE: CORE outcome measures.

Conclusion

We have found this intervention to be supportive of young people, easy for facilitators to follow, and beneficial to the young people themselves. More detail on these issues is provided in *Supporting Young People with Anxiety: A Practical Guide* (Herrick & Redman-White, 2019).

We are confident you will find this workbook a useful addition to your resources bank. We would welcome any feedback you could provide to ensure that our work goes on growing and improving. Please respond to:

liz@lizherrick.co.uk
barbarahrw@gmail.com

Thank you for considering this resource; we hope you will find it as successful as we have.

References

Assessment Questionnaires Available Online

CORE-10 (10 items; Age 18+). www.coresystemtrust.org.uk/instruments/core-10-information/
Generalised Anxiety Disorder (7 items; Ages 11–17). https://www.mdcalc.com/calc/1727/gad7-general-anxiety-disorder
Generalised Anxiety Disorder (7 items; Age 18+). file:///C:/Users/home/Downloads/APA_DSM5_Level-2-Anxiety-Adult.pdf
Goodman, R., et al. (2003). Strengths and Difficulties Questionnaire, (25 Items; Versions for ages 11–17 and 18+). https://sdqinfo.org/
Revised Children's Scale of Anxiety and Depression (47 items; Ages 8–18). Available at https://www.childfirst.ucla.edu/publications/
YP-CORE: CORE outcome measures, (10 items; Ages 13–17). www.coresystemtrust.org.uk/instruments/yp-core-information/

Books

Herrick, E., and Redman-White, B. (2019). *Supporting Young People with Anxiety: A Practical Guide*. Routledge.

Conference Presentation

Hadwin, J., Herrick, E., Redman-White, B. (2020). *Supporting Children and Young People with Anxiety: A Pilot Study*, Presented at BPS/DECP Annual Conference, January 2020 (unpublished but available from authors.)

Session 1 Understanding Anxiety

Facilitator Notes

Session Aims

In the first session, we aim to welcome students to the group, help them feel comfortable and understand more about the course. We will explain how the group will work and what types of activities they will be involved in. An icebreaker game is provided to help students feel at ease and start to get to know each other. We aim to introduce students to understanding that the way we respond in any situation comprises four parts: physiology, thoughts, feelings, and behaviour. This will be reinforced throughout the course.

We will begin to look at what happens to us when we are anxious and to understand that anxiety is a normal response. The fight/flight/freeze model will be discussed to help with the understanding of anxiety. Students will be encouraged to think about their own personal goals for the course.

Theory

The model being used is based on the four-way interaction between thoughts, emotions, behaviours, and physiology (Herrick & Redman-White, 2019). This includes the cognitive behaviour model (CBT) and extends recent findings from trauma-based work by Bessel van der Kolk et al. 'The Body Keeps the Score' 2014 on the importance of stored memories in the body. An evolutionary theory of the purpose of anxiety and how it affects the body is adopted.

Learning Points

Our responses comprise the interaction amongst actions, thoughts, emotions, and bodily feelings. They are all interconnected, and a change in one will affect the others. We have evolved with emotions to keep us safe. Anxiety is a powerful emotion related to fear which protects us from harm.
The fight/flight/freeze response is activated when we feel anxious, resulting in changes which interrupt our logical thinking processes. To think clearly, we need to reduce the physical effect of the fear response by making changes to our bodily state.

Many of us are already doing things to help ourselves, and it is useful to start by recognising steps we have already taken. Sharing our own strategies may also be helpful to others in the group.

Authors' Note

The first session is a little more complex to organise than the following sessions as the group rules need to be agreed, personal goals set, and an overview of the programme given. Please bear with us; the subsequent sessions will be easier to organise.

References

Herrick, E., and Redman-White, B. (2019). *Supporting Children and Young People With Anxiety*, Chapter 1. Routledge.
van der Kolk, B. (2014). *The Body Keeps the Score*. Penguin.

DOI:10.4324/9781003180364-1

Script

Resources

YouTube video
https://www.youtube.com/watch?v=rpolpKTWrp4&t=7s
"Anxiety Explained for Teens"

Main learning points of the video:

- Anxiety is a normal response to a threat.
- The fight/flight/freeze response is an evolutionary survival mechanism.
- There are different parts of the brain involved in survival.
- Problem solving.

Coloured tokens: e.g., counters, cards, etc.

Handouts

1.1   Interactive Model
1.2   Our Group Rules (one for each student to sign)
1.3   Personal Goals (one per student)
1.4   Positive Diary (optional – students may prefer to use their phones)

Purpose and Resources Required	*Plan*
Introduction	
Facilitator to introduce self and explain how the group will work	Introduce self and explain practical details of how the group will work, including:
	• When/where meetings will take place
	• Structure and content of the sessions, including
	o information
	o discussion
	o activities
	o video clips
	o relaxation techniques
	o practice tasks
Teaching	
Explanation of the model being used	*What we do is a result of the interaction between our thoughts, emotions, physical feelings, and behaviour.*
	Changing one aspect can change the others.
Interaction between thoughts, behaviour, emotions, and physiology	*We will identify strategies that help us to cope better.*
	Provide:
	Handout 1.1: Illustration of the model
Handout 1.1 Interactive Model	Give examples of interactions and ask students to think of some more.

Purpose and Resources Required	*Plan*
Activity	
Icebreaker, group introductions	Produce coloured tokens.
Coloured tokens	Allow all students to take a few.
	Ask getting-to-know-you questions to be answered by students with a coloured token. If the students do not already know each other's names, they can start their answer with "My name is X and . . ."
	For example:
	If you have a blue token, answer this question: Do you have a pet at home?
	Each student with a blue token answers, "My name is X, and I have a dog," or "My name is X, and I don't have pets."
	If you have a yellow token: "What is your favourite colour?"
	Keep it simple and short.
	Alternative suggestions:
	What is your favourite food?
	What type of music do you enjoy?
	Do you play any sports?
	What is your favourite television programme/video game?
Ground Rules	
Handout 1.2: Our Group Rules.	The group/ground rules need to be established. Discuss and agree on four or five group rules that everyone is happy with.
	Suggest some rules to get the group started:
	• Listening to each other
	• Ensuring what we say in the group stays in the group
	• Trying to say helpful things to each other
	Others may include trying to be honest or joining in as much as possible.
	Capture them on your electronic screen/whiteboard or on paper and have students sign a copy.
Personal Goals	
Handout 1.3: Personal Goals	Provide Handout 1.3: Personal Goals.
	Discuss the importance of setting realistic and manageable goals, which include what the students would like to able to do differently after working with the group.
	Remember that these will be re-visited later in the course, to see what we have learnt. Try to keep them safe.
	The facilitator may want to keep copies of the goals in case students misplace or forget them. They will be needed again in Session 10.
Teaching	*Anxiety is the feeling that goes with fear. Fear is a NORMAL emotion which has developed to keep us safe.*
Understanding the anxiety response	*We all experience anxiety, and we will never be completely free of anxiety, nor would we want to be. In the right amount at the right time, anxiety is a helpful emotion that keeps us safe.*
Emphasising that anxiety is normal	*Anxiety is only a problem when we have too much of it, or it comes at the wrong times or for things that don't need us to be anxious.*
	We can learn how to manage stress and anxiety so that it does not interfere with our everyday lives.

Purpose and Resources Required	*Plan*
Teaching The fight/flight/freeze response	*The fight/flight/freeze response comes from the part of our brains that deals with emotions, which has been present from our early beginnings. It sits deep in the middle of the brain and is called the amygdala.*
Teaching Evolutionary understanding of our responses	*To survive as a species, we need to be alert to physical threats.* *Fear evolved to alert us to danger and make us fight back, run away, or hide. This is called the fight/flight/freeze response.* *When we are in danger, the emotional part of the brain (amygdala) acts as a "anxiety alarm" and goes off to alert us to danger (a bit like a smoke alarm). When this part of the brain is activated, our bodies produce hormones and chemicals which give us strength and speed. At this time, it is difficult for our thinking brain (cortex) to engage effectively.*
Activity Fight/flight/freeze video: "Anxiety Explained for Teens"	Show video: https://www.youtube.com/watch?v=rpolpKTWrp4&t=7s "Anxiety Explained for Teens" Have students talk in pairs/small groups about situations/people/activities that create anxiety for them. Ask for feedback.
Discussion Identification of coping strategies already being used Helping students feel they have some skills already	*Do others get anxious: parents, teachers, friends?* *Does everyone become anxious about the same things?* *Does anyone have ideas about what helps them when they feel worried?* *Does anyone use any apps that they find useful in managing their anxiety? If so, what are they, and how do they help?* Capture on electronic screen/whiteboard to consider later.
Conclusion Review of main learning points from the session	Review: Thoughts, feelings, behaviours, and physiology interact. Anxiety is a normal response that we all experience. Awareness of the fight/flight/freeze response. Different parts of the brain are activated when we are anxious; the anxiety alarm takes over from rational thinking.
Grounding Exercise Feeling positive when finishing the session	*To help us switch off the anxiety alarm and return to rational thinking, we need to help our bodies relax and think positively.* *What are you looking forward to over the next few days?* *What are you going to do that will be fun?* Discuss.

Purpose and Resources Required	*Plan*

Practice Task

Handout 1.4: Positive Diary

Fill in the diary sheet identifying things that have gone well during the day. If you prefer, you can make notes on your phone.

Often, identifying things that are going well helps us feel more positive and enjoy life more.

What would be a good time of day for you to fill this in? Would it be helpful to do it the same time every day?

What might get in the way of you completing this task?

We will be discussing the positive experiences you have this week at the beginning of the next session.

Relaxation Exercise

Diaphragmatic breathing/belly breathing

We are going to practise one of our relaxation exercises —diaphragmatic breathing, sometimes called belly breathing.

To begin to help students find ways of switching off their anxiety alarm

When we breathe consciously and deeply into our lungs, our bodies start to relax, oxygen reaches more parts of the body and brain, and the nervous system shifts out of the fight/flight/freeze response.

Exhaling through the mouth for longer than inhaling is an important aspect of this exercise.

Concentrate on your breathing for five breaths. If your mind wanders off, just gently bring it back to noticing your breathing.

Now we are going to change the rhythm of our breathing slightly. Breathe in through your nose to the count of four or five, then breath out through your mouth for a count of six or seven. Repeat five times.

Pushing your stomach out as you breathe in and pulling it in as you breathe out are important to expand the lungs as much as possible.

As you breathe in, push your belly out. Put your hand on your belly and feel it expand as you breathe. This pushes the diaphragm down so that more air fills the lungs.

How was that for everyone? Let's each try again on our own.

Allow a minute for practice.

Try it out during the week and see if it helps.

Have a great week everyone, I look forward to seeing you at our next session.

It can feel counterintuitive and may need practising.

1.1 Interactive Model

These factors are all related, changing one of them will change the others.

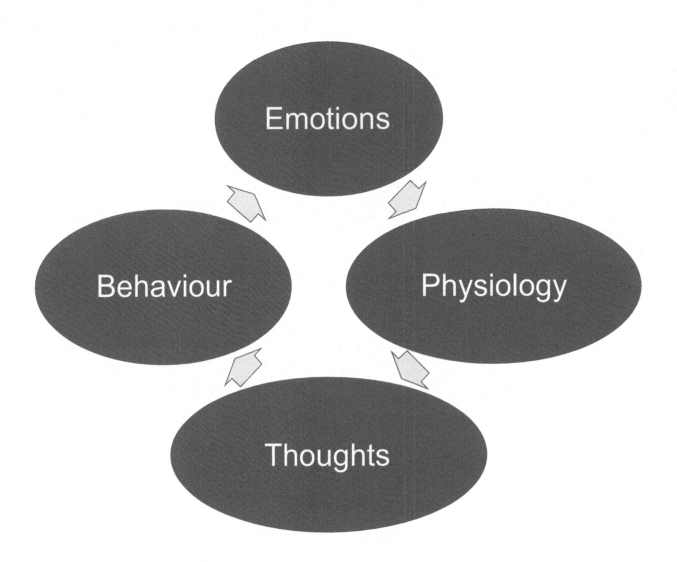

1.2 Group Rules

Our Group Rules

- Confidentiality outside the group, as discussed and explained regarding safeguarding concerns.

- Listen carefully and respectfully to what everyone has to say.

Be open to new things and ideas (whilst accepting that everything might not work for you).

Rules Agreed by the Group:

-

-

-

-

-

Signed:

1.3 Personal Goals

Think about what you would like to gain by attending these sessions.

I would like to understand and know more about . . . ☐ My behaviour ☐ My feelings ☐ My physiology ☐ My thoughts and emotions ☐ Relaxation/breathing techniques ☐ Self-belief	**I would like to learn how to . . .** **This will help me because . . .** **I will know that I have achieved this when . . .**
I would like to be able to . . . **This will help me because . . .** **I will know when I have achieved this when . . .**	**After I have completed these sessions, I hope that I continue to . . .** I can't do it
Other things that are important to me during these sessions are . . .	

Your goals need to be realistic and manageable for the duration of this group.

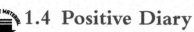

1.4 Positive Diary

Please bring the completed sheet back with you or make a note on your phone as this will be discussed at the next session.

What Went Well This Week?

Write down the best thing that happens to you each day; it doesn't matter how big or small the event is.

Day	What Went Well	Time of Day (Morning, Afternoon, or Evening)
Monday		
Tuesday		
Wednesday		
Thursday		
Friday		
Saturday		
Sunday		

Session 2 Helpful/Unhelpful Coping Strategies

Facilitator Notes

Session Aims

The aim of this second session is to explore the steps that are already being taken by the young people to address their issues. Students will be taught how to distinguish between maladaptive (unhelpful) strategies, such as avoidance, self-harm, and excessive alcohol use and adaptive (helpful) strategies, such as exercise and relaxation techniques. The purpose and effectiveness of the helpful strategies will be discussed, and they will be reinforced as the better strategies. The harmful effects of the unhelpful strategies will also be discussed to help students realise why they do not work in the long term.

Perfectionism is discussed as it is often associated with anxiety and stress in young people and is seen as being likely to lead to unhelpful coping strategies.

Theory

The solution-focused brief therapy approach (see De Shazer 1988; Ratner et al., 2012) assumes that everyone is trying to improve their situation, but they might not have the tools required to be successful. Recognising efforts already being made validates the person and allows the helping professional to recognise their strengths. Reinforcing positive action already being taken has the advantage that, by definition, the person has those skills in their repertoire even if they are not always used. This increases the likelihood that the young person will be able to put helpful plans into action.

Learning Points

We all have limits on the amount of stress we can easily cope with; some have greater tolerance than others. However, there are opportunities to change either our situation or our way of dealing with it so that we are not overwhelmed. The analogy of a bucket (our capacity for stress) being filled with water (stress) is used. We may not be able to change the size of our "bucket," but we can create "taps" to release the water. Some "taps" are genuinely helpful in reducing stress that leads to anxiety; others appear helpful at the time but cause ongoing issues later.

References

De Shazer, S. (1988). *Clues: Investigating Solutions in Brief Therapy*. W. W. Norton & Co.

Ratner, H., George, E., and Iveson, C. (2012). *Solution Focused Brief Therapy: 100 Key Points and Techniques*. Routledge.

DOI:10.4324/9781003180364-2

Script

Resources

YouTube video
www.youtube.com/watch?v=CZTc8_FwHGM
"How Stress Affects Your Body and Mind"

Main learning points of this video:

- Understanding the importance of maintaining our stress levels within healthy limits
- The effects of too much stress
- Examples of strategies that help reduce stress and those that increase levels of stress over time
- The difference between short-term relief and long-term benefits

YouTube video
www.youtube.com/watch?v=LySC3v5geAc
"Stop Trying to be Perfect"

Main learning points of this video:

- Trying to be perfect is an impossible task.
- To be human is to be imperfect.
- Setting unrealistic goals usually leads to feelings of failure and increases anxiety and stress.

Optional video
www.youtube.com/watch?v=MoQVgJx_QN4&t=34s
"Grounding Exercise for Anxiety #10: Square Breathing"

Handouts

2.1   The Stress Bucket, positive and negative strategies
2.2   Thinking About My Personal Strategies
2.3   Thinking About New Strategies

Purpose and Resources Required	*Plan*
Introduction	
Welcome	Demonstrate appreciation that the students have returned for another session.
Our Group Rules (agreed last time)	Display the rules agreed last session and remind all students of them.
Review	Discuss the practice task.
Session 2 Content	*Did you manage to keep a record of positive things that happened throughout the week?*
	Ask students to share one example, either in pairs or to the group, depending on confidence levels.
	Was this diary helpful? How did it make you feel? Is it something you would do more of?
	Encourage discussion.
	What about the breathing technique; did anyone try it?
	Let's have one more practice to remind ourselves.
	In this session, we are going to talk about the things we do when we are stressed. Some of these things can be really helpful; others seem to be helpful in the short term but cause us more stress in the end.
	Perfectionism will also be considered in more detail.

Purpose and Resources Required	*Plan*
Icebreaker	In threes or fours, give students four or five minutes to find three things they have in common – the weirder the better!
Teaching Explain the difference between helpful and unhelpful coping strategies that we use when we are anxious. Video: "How Stress Affects your Body and Mind"	Show video: www.youtube.com/watch?v=CZTc8_FwHGM "How Stress Affects your Body and Mind"
Discussion Emphasise the importance of stress and when/how it changes from helpful to unhelpful. Identify short-term and long-term strategies	*What did you think of the video?* • *Do you find the analogy of our tolerance for stress being a bucket helpful?* • *Do you think that is right – that we each have a different-size bucket?* • *What about the analogy of strategies to help being taps that can reduce the water (stress) level?* Ask students to identify behaviours that they think are short-term "quick fixes" to stress and those that work in the long term. Discuss in pairs, then share in the group.
Teaching Introduce the concept of perfectionism. Video: "Stop Trying to be Perfect"	*Perfectionism arises from trying to live up to an idealised version of ourselves. Perfectionism increases anxiety and stress as it is unattainable.* *It can also paralyse motivation to work for fear of "not doing well enough."* Show video: www.youtube.com/watch?v=LySC3v5geAc "Stop Trying to be Perfect" *How many of you have felt the need to be perfect?* *What effect does that have on your performance?* *Does it help?* *Where do these pressures come from?*
Activity Handout 2.1: The Stress Bucket This activity helps us apply the concepts we discussed to our own behaviour and those of others we know. Handout 2.2: Thinking About My Personal Strategies	Provide Handouts 2.1 and 2.2 and allow time for reflection and filling them in. Depending on the group, it might be possible for people to share what they have written on the worksheets, or it might be better to allow people to keep it to themselves. If the facilitator offers the opportunity to share, be sure to say that everyone has the right to pass.

Purpose and Resources Required	*Plan*
Conclusion Review of main learning points from this session	*This week we have considered:* • *Individual differences in how much stress we tolerate easily* • *The difference between short-term strategies that lead to more stress and helpful strategies that keep us healthy over the long term* • *The difficulties associated with perfectionism*
Practice Task: Reinforcing positive personal strategies Handout 2.3: Thinking About New Strategies	*Anxiety can be difficult to manage, especially when it is extreme. It is tempting to do things that will make us feel better quickly to get rid of the discomfort.* *Some of those behaviours can be harmful in the long run.* *We are starting to learn that there are some simple changes we can make that will help us feel better over time.* *Our aim is for each of us to develop a tool kit of strategies that we can dip into when we need to.* *For next week I would like you to complete Handout 2.3 Thinking about new strategies or, if you are ready to give something a go right away, choose one of the helpful things you have identified today, make a note of it on your phone or on paper, and practice it during the week.* *Keep a note of:* • *When* • *Where* • *How often* • *How helpful it was* *We will come back and discuss this at the beginning of the next session.*
Relaxation Exercise Square breathing A second breathing exercise that some people may prefer to the one we tried last week Video: "Grounding Exercise for Anxiety #10: Square Breathing"	*Square breathing:* • *Close your eyes and relax your body.* • *Breathe in for a count of four.* • *Hold the breath for a count of four.* • *Breathe out for a count of four.* • *Hold the breath for a count of four.* *The first time, I will count for you.* Leave a one-second gap between numbers. *In . . . two . . . three . . . four . . .* *Hold . . .two . . . three . . . four . . .* *Out . . . two . . . three . . . four . . .* *Hold . . . two . . . three . . . four . . .* *Now try it on your own four more times.* *Some people find it helpful to imagine a square as they do this, with each side being either a breath or a hold of breath. You might even wish to draw this in the air as you breathe.* Show video: www.youtube.com/watch?v=MoQVgJx_QN4&t=34s "Grounding Exercise for Anxiety #10: Square Breathing" The first two and a half minutes describe basic square breathing, which is sufficient for most purposes. *Any questions from today's session?* *Time to finish. Look forward to seeing you all in the next session.*

2.1 The Stress Bucket

How Big is My Stress Bucket?

Tick the box under the bucket which is the best metaphorical bucket for your stress capacity.

☐   ☐   ☐   ☐

I chose this bucket because . . .

2.2 Thinking About My Personal Strategies

Look at the different coping strategies shown in the chart. Think carefully about whether you currently use them **never**, **sometimes**, or **regularly** when you are stressed. Shade in the box which is most appropriate for each strategy.

		Regularly	**Sometimes**	**Never**
Effective Coping Strategies	Problem solving			
	Exercise			
	Quality sleep			
	Relaxation			
	Sharing your feelings			
Unhelpful Coping Strategies	Staying up late			
	Sleeping in			
	Drugs/alcohol/comfort eating			
	Inactivity			
	Procrastination			
	Suppressing/ignoring problems			

2.3 Thinking About New Strategies

Now think about which strategies could be a more effective way of coping with the stressors and anxieties that you feel. Describe situations when you might usually feel stressed.

Situation	Strategy You Would Normally Use	Strategy You Will Try Next Time	How You Think This New Strategy Will Help You

Session 3 How Anxiety Makes Our Bodies Feel

Facilitator Notes

Session Aims

In the third session, the aim is for students to be able to identify, recognise, and normalise the physical feelings we have in our bodies when we feel anxious. We want students to be able to recognise that these feelings can be varied and that whilst they are felt physically, they arise from emotional roots. Physical sensations in the body arise before we can think about being worried and can help us recognise that we are anxious.

The importance of reducing the level of physiological arousal will be emphasised through breathing and relaxation techniques practised in each session.

Theory

A neuro-physiological approach to understanding the arousal system is employed (Herrick & Redman-White, 2019).

Learning Points

It is important to understand that the physiological responses of anxiety result from the fight/flight/freeze response in our bodies. Recognising that, although it may feel like we are physically unwell, it is a temporary state that can be changed to help us feel more in control and stop us feeling concerned about it (Fletcher, 2014). We will stress the importance of recognising and changing our own levels of physiological arousal in order to help us stay calm and rational and reduce our levels of threat.

References

Fletcher, J. (2014). *Anxiety, Panicking about Panic*. Amazon Publications.
Herrick, E., and Redman-White, B. (2019). *Supporting Children and Young People With Anxiety*. Routledge.

DOI:10.4324/9781003180364-3

Script

Resources

YouTube video:
www.youtube.com/watch?v=vdzAM8mKad8
"Anxiety and Physical Symptoms"

Main learning points of the video:
• Physical reactions to anxiety and stress are felt in our bodies and do not reflect physical ill health.
• A wide range of physical reactions may be experienced.
• We may all experience a different set of physical reactions to anxiety.

Handouts

3.1   Common Physical Reactions to Stress
3.2   Body Template
3.3   Physical Reactions Diary

Purpose and Resources Required	*Plan*
Introduction	
Welcome	Welcome students back and appreciate their continuing involvement.
Review and Rules	Give a reminder of the group rules. Check if the rules are working or if they need any adjustment to be negotiated.
	Does anyone have any questions from the last session that you thought of later?
	Allow discussion.
	How did the practice task go?
	• *What did you note down in your phones/on paper?*
	• *Let's share strategies that worked and those that didn't.*
	Discuss.
	Record strategies that work for students.
	Discuss the square breathing relaxation exercise:
	• Practised?
	• Helpful?
	• Comments?
	• More effective than Session 1 breathing?
Icebreaker Pass the Word	A real or imaginary ball can be used for this game. The first person holds the ball and says aloud the first word that comes into their head (e.g., "apple"). Then they throw the ball to the next person who says the first word they think of (e.g., "banana"). The ball is passed until everyone has been included. Go around two or three times or throw to random group members. The last person throws the ball to the facilitator. The facilitator then explains that our thoughts are affected by previous connections. We can get into habits in our thinking: some useful and some not helpful in managing our anxiety.

Purpose and Resources Required	*Plan*
Session 3 Content	*This week, we are going to consider how anxiety makes our bodies feel.* • *There is a wide range of physical feelings, depending on the individual.* • *All of us are different.* • *We can recognise that we are anxious and worried by noticing what is happening in our bodies.*
Activity This activity demonstrates that we are all individuals and that we "hear" and interpret things using our previously learnt experiences.	Provide each student with a sheet of paper. Ask students to close their eyes and listen to the instructions being given by the facilitator. They are not allowed to ask questions during the activity. Give these directions (facilitator does the activity too): • *Fold the sheet of paper in half.* • *Fold the paper in half again.* • *Now tear off the lower right-hand corner of the sheet.* • *Tear off the upper right-hand corner.* • *Fold the paper in half again.* • *Tear off the upper left-hand corner.* *Now open your eyes, and let's see what we have.* Discuss differences in the outcomes of this activity.
Teaching	*As you can see, some of us have interpreted the same instructions differently. This does not make us "right" or "wrong" but shows that our previous learnt experiences have influenced how we have "heard" the instructions and put them into practice.* *When our amygdala (anxiety alarm) is set off, this produces a range of physiological changes in our bodies.* *We have learnt over time that when we have pain or discomfort in our bodies, it can be associated with physical illness, so it is easy to interpret any physical changes as symptoms of "being ill."* *Sometimes, of course, that is right – we have a stomach upset or flu.* *At other times, it is anxiety that gives us the stomach upset, shakes, or other physical symptoms.* *Can anyone describe a time that happened to them, or they noticed it in somebody else?*
Activity Handout 3.1: Common Physical Reactions to Stress	Brainstorm the physical changes that that we have experienced in our bodies. Facilitator may wish to record them on the screen. Give out Handout 3.1. *Did we miss any? Does anyone recognise one they forgot to mention?*

Purpose and Resources Required	Plan
Teaching	*The physical changes may be the first clue we get that we need to do something differently. Getting better at identifying and recognising these physical feelings can help us find ways to make ourselves feel better before our feelings take control of our behaviours.*
	Accepting and understanding that we are having a physical response to anxiety can help us manage it better.
	Finding ways to relax and calm can send more oxygen to the thinking part of the brain and calm the nervous system so that we can evaluate whether there is real danger or not. Coughing and sighing are good examples of the importance of exhaling to calm our nervous system.
	That is why every session will finish with a relaxation technique as this is the first step to helping us feel calmer.
Activity Video: "Anxiety and Physical Symptoms"	Show video: www.youtube.com/watch?v=vdzAM8mKad8 "Anxiety and Physical Symptoms" Show all or a selected part of the video to demonstrate some of the range of physical symptoms.
Discussion	• *Which of your own physical reactions did you recognise from the video?*
	• *Which were surprising to you?*
Activity Handout 3.2: Body Template	Give out the handout of a body template. Ask the students to draw and label on the template their own physical reactions to stress.
	What have we learnt today?
	Discuss.
Conclusion	*Main learning points:*
	• *Our bodies may notice our anxiety before we become conscious of it.*
	• *We may think we are ill.*
	• *Understanding our own body's reaction to anxiety is important in helping us recognise and manage it.*
Practice Task Handout 3.3: Physical Reactions Diary	*Before the next session, try and become consciously aware of any physical reactions that suggest to you that you are anxious.*
	Record them for discussion next time.
	Provide Handout 3.3
	You can use this sheet or, if you prefer, record on your phone.

Purpose and Resources Required	*Plan*

Relaxation Exercise:

Five-Minute De-stress Activity	*Make sure you are sitting comfortably: uncross your legs, relax your arms, and close your eyes.*
	Think about your breathing; notice it coming and going through your nose.
	Allow time for seven to ten breaths.
	Notice any tension in your body. Allow yourself to let go of any tension in your shoulders . . . neck . . . jaw . . . hands . . . fingers . . .
	Give a little time for each part of the body.
	Notice any tension in your stomach and allow it to drop away . . . Do the same for your back . . . buttocks . . . and feet . . . Allow all tension to drop away.
	Move your attention to your chest, slow your breaths to become more regular and deeper . . . and then let go with a large exhale.
	Imagine your next activity.
	Now smile and enjoy feeling relaxed.
	When you are ready open your eyes and feel prepared for your next activity.
	Have a great week everyone. I look forward to seeing you at our next session.

3.1 Common Physical Reactions to Stress

Here is a list of the most commonly felt physical reactions when we are anxious and stressed.

Our bodies are helping us prepare for danger. What we experience is:

- Faster breathing, rapid heartbeat: providing oxygen to the muscles
- Discomfort in our stomach, dry mouth: digestive system shuts down
- Sweating: to cool us down
- Tense muscles: ready for action
- Elevated blood pressure: to pump blood to muscles when needed
- Pupils dilated: to let in more light
- Eyes wide open and eyebrows raised: to see more effectively
- Nostrils flare: to take in extra air and smell more effectively
- A fuzzy head, lack of clear thinking: to take action and not think

This energy boost can lead to uncomfortable physical feelings in our bodies. This may even make people feel that they are ill:

- Trembling
- Shaking
- Feeling twitchy
- Heart beating fast/felt as a pounding in the chest
- Feeling like something is stuck in your throat
- Dizziness
- Headache
- Stomach ache
- Diarrhoea
- Nausea and sickness
- Breathlessness
- Chest pain

It is important, of course, to check with your GP that there are no physical difficulties that may be contributing to any symptoms you are experiencing.

3.2 Body Template

Label/draw where you feel your emotions in your body when you are anxious.

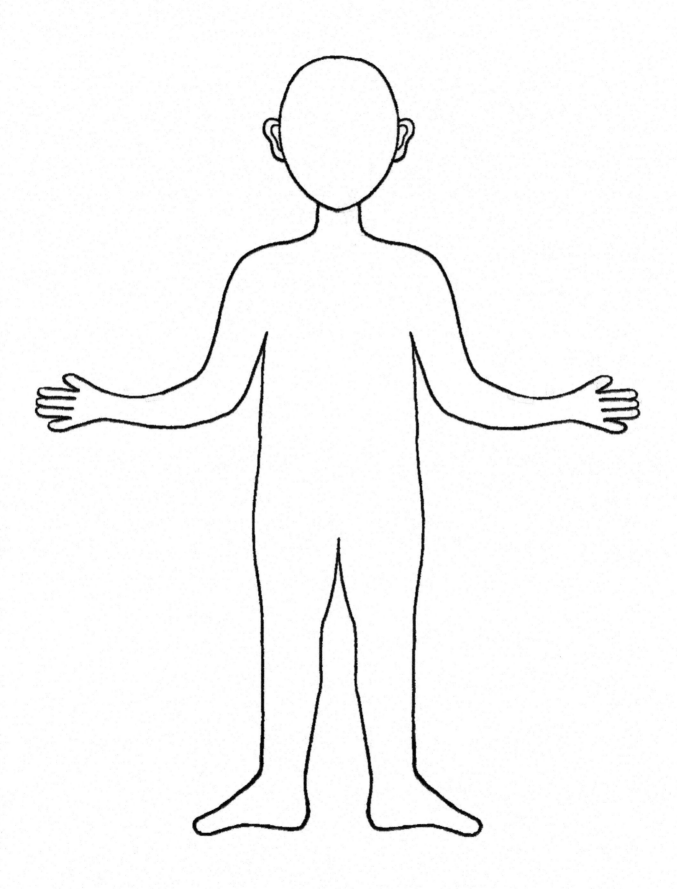

3.3 Physical Reactions Diary

Record any physical feelings of anxiety/stress that you have during this week. Notice what activity was causing you stress or anxiety at the time.

Day	What Was Happening at the Time?	Which Physical Feelings Did You Experience?	What Did You Do to Calm These Feelings?
Monday			
Tuesday			
Wednesday			
Thursday			
Friday			
Saturday			
Sunday			

Session 4 Understanding and Managing Our Emotions

Facilitator Notes

Session Aims

This session aims to help young people understand the importance of recognising, understanding and expressing emotions appropriately. They will learn that emotions give us important information, but it is perfectly normal to find it difficult to talk about them. Students learn that emotions are felt in their body before their rational brain decides the most appropriate course of action. This can lead to actions being "hijacked" by emotions. This means that we behave in ways that are out of the control of our rational thought. These behaviours tend to be spontaneous, unwanted, and unhelpful for effective communication. Students are also introduced to another relaxation method.

Theory

Emotions are one of the four aspects of the model we are using. (The others are behaviour, thoughts, and physiology). Recognising, understanding, and regulating our emotions is crucial to managing our thoughts and behaviours (Damasio, 2000). If emotions are not recognised, named, and understood, they may interfere with rational thinking and make us behave in ways that are not in our interests (Guarino, 2015). We are introducing the term "hijack" as shorthand for times when our attempts to change thoughts and behaviours are made difficult or prevented by unhelpful emotions.

Learning Points

Emotions cause physiological changes that can be felt in the body.
  Emotions are important because:

- They give us important information.
- They help us to communicate with each other.
- They motivate us to act in certain ways.
- They can be enjoyable.

Difficulties can arise when:

- They get out of balance (i.e., switched off or overwhelming).
- They conflict with our thoughts.
- They get displaced.
- They can be unpleasant to experience.

References

Damasio, A. (2000). *The Feelings of What Happens.* Vintage Books.
Guarino, R. (2015). *Me and My Feelings: What Emotions Are and How We Can Manage Them,* Hoopoe Books.

DOI:10.4324/9781003180364-4

Script

Resources

YouTube video:
www.youtube.com/watch?v=VL5MvZKgVZA&t=14s
"Identifying Our Feelings"

Main learning points of the video:
• Understanding the characteristics of emotions: e.g. sudden, provide information, neither good nor bad
• Recognising and naming different emotions

Game

Recognising Emotions (Ensure these are cut into individual cards before the session; you may want to print them on card and/or laminate them.)

Handouts

4.1   Emotional Vocabulary Table
4.2   Emotions Cards for Game

Purpose and Resources Required	Plan
Introduction	
Welcome	Welcome students to this session; appreciate that they are taking the time and commitment to continue.
Group Rules	Remind them of the rules if you think this is still necessary.
Review	
Session 4 Content	*Your practice task was to notice physical reactions in your body. What did you notice?* Discuss.
	Does it help to know that these reactions are "normal" and that we all experience them to a greater or lesser extent?
	How did you find the task last week?
	Did you find it easy to be aware of your physical reactions?
	Did anyone notice anything new?
	In this session, we are going to consider our emotions. They are closely linked to and contribute to the physical feelings in our bodies.
	Remind students of the original model: responses are a result of the interactions of actions, thoughts, emotions, and physiology.
	Revisit if necessary.
Icebreaker	Choose any everyday object in the room (a paper clip, a doorknob, a stapler, a backpack, etc.) Ask everyone to come up with as many possible uses for the item as they can.
	The rules of brainstorming are:
	• *We are going for quantity not quality of ideas at this point.*
	• *The more ideas the better.*
	• *No one is to judge or criticise; there are no wrong suggestions.*
	• *Build on each other's ideas.*

Purpose and Resources Required	Plan
Activity	*I am going to ask you to close your eyes for one minute, (or think silently if you don't wish to close your eyes) and remember a really good experience you have had. This may have been alone or with family and friends.* Pause for a minute. *Who would like to share their experience and how it felt?* (Facilitator to share one if it is helpful.) Discuss which of these descriptions are **physical** (e.g., calm, relaxed), **thoughts** (e.g., It was beautiful), **emotions** (e.g., content, excited). Relate to the model revisited in the Introduction.
Teaching	*We all have emotions. While different things may make each of us happy and sad, we all experience happiness and sadness. Emotions give us information and help keep us safe (just like fear/anxiety).* *We sometimes find it difficult to talk about our emotions. They can be seen as bad or embarrassing. Feeling our emotions can also be physically uncomfortable at times.* *This can lead to us bottling up our emotions. However, when we are not in touch with our emotions, we are in danger of not experiencing joy and happiness.*
Discussion Video: "Identify Your Feelings"	Show video: https://www.youtube.com/watch?v=VL5MvZKgVZA&t=14s "Identify Your Feelings" Discuss the issues arising from the video and how they relate to the students. Consider the issues within a school and home context.
Teaching Handout 4.1: Emotional Vocabulary Table	*The five basic emotions are recognised as:* • *Sadness* • *Disgust* • *Fear* • *Anger* • *Happiness* *There are, however, many more: e.g., surprise, disappointment, frustration.* *What emotions are you aware of experiencing?* Note them down on paper/personal whiteboards. Handout 4.1 Emotional Vocabulary Table. Ask students if they recognise any more feelings from the worksheet that they have not already noted down.
Activity Handout 4.2: Emotions Cards for Game (previously cut out)	*Most of our emotions are expressed through our facial features and our body language.* *It is sometimes easier to recognise other people's emotions than it is our own.* *I am going to give out some cards with emotions written on them. Take one but keep it face down and don't show it to anyone else. Now look at it yourself.* *Take it in turns to give the rest of the group clues to recognise what the emotion on the card is, without using the word. You can talk, act, or mime.* Depending on the maturity of the students, you might choose either simpler or more complex emotions for the students to describe/act.

Purpose and Resources Required	Plan
Teaching	*Emotions are felt first in our bodies before our rational brain labels them or decides what to do next. Emotions provide us with motivation to act/behave in particular ways.*
	Emotions themselves are neither good nor bad. We might think some emotions are "better" than others, but it is our behaviour that may be helpful or unhelpful to ourselves and others. Emotions may be uncomfortable feelings that we want to change or pleasant ones that we want to enjoy.
	Sometimes our emotions "leak out" and lead us to behave in ways we regret afterwards.
	Give an example from your own experience.
	We call this being "hijacked" by our emotions as often we end up doing things we regret later.
Discussion	In pairs or, if a small group, within the whole group, talk about ways in which you, or people you know, may have acted that reflected unrecognised feelings (i.e., been "hijacked").
	Examples usually reflect our fight/flight responses, saying something we regret, lashing out at someone or something, withdrawing, avoiding situations.
Conclusion	*The main learning points I want you to take away from the session are:*
	• *Recognising our emotions is important.*
	• *They are sometimes difficult to talk about.*
	• *There are no bad emotions — only bad actions.*
	• *Emotions give us information and help us communicate.*
	• *If not recognised and expressed, they may "leak out" and lead to us to actions we regret later.*
Relaxation Exercise Calm Place	*This exercise can help your brain take a break from whatever stress you are experiencing.*
	Start with three breaths, either diaphragmatic/belly or square breathing, whichever you found best for you.
	Close your eyes (or keep open if student feels uncomfortable).
	Visualise a place where you have experienced being calm and relaxed: your "calm place."
	It could be a cabin in the woods, a sandy beach, a room in your house, or a mountain path.
	Notice how it looks, feels, smells, and sounds — the more details the better.
	Notice what emotions you feel when you are in your calm place.
	Allow five minutes for this activity.
	Give your calm place a name.
	Would anyone like to share?
	No pressure if not; it is the exercise that matters, not the sharing.
Practice Task	*Draw and/or write about your calm place.*
	Find a quiet place and try to go to your calm place two or three times in the week.
	Notice what emotions you feel when you are in your calm place.
	Thank you for your hard work today.
	Take care. I look forward to seeing you at the next session.

4.1 Emotional Vocabulary Table

Angry	Sad	Anxious	Hurt	Embarrassed	Happy
grumpy	disappointed	afraid	jealous	self-conscious	thankful
frustrated	mournful	stressed	betrayed	lonely	trusting
annoyed	regretful	vulnerable	isolated	inferior	comfortable
defensive	depressed	confused	deprived	guilty	content
spiteful	paralysed	bewildered	victimised	ashamed	excited
impatient	pessimistic	worried	aggrieved	pathetic	relaxed
offended	tearful	cautious	bullied	confused	confident
irritated	dismayed	nervous	abandoned	different	relieved

4.2 Emotions Cards for the Game

Recognising Emotions

Prior to the session, you will need to photocopy and cut into individual cards.

Admiration	**Adoration**	**Appreciation**
Anger	**Anxiety**	**Awe**
Awkwardness	**Boredom**	**Calm**
Confusion	**Craving**	**Sadness**

Disgust	**Pain**	**Envy**
Excitement	**Fear**	**Frustration**
Happiness	**Horror**	**Interest**
Pride	**Romantic Attraction**	**Sadness**
Satisfaction	**Shame**	**Sympathy**

Session 5 Changing Our Thoughts

Facilitator Notes

Session Aims

In this session, we aim to help students identify the thought styles that increase and maintain anxiety. This then reinforces the importance of the relationship between how we think, feel, and behave. We encourage students to consider the effect of negative self-talk and include some basic neurophysiology. The importance of individual perceptions and alternative ways of thinking about situations is the main emphasis of this session (Seligman, 2011).

Theory

Cognitive behavioural approaches and neuroscience are employed in this session. Cognitive behavioural approaches make use of the links between thoughts, feelings, and behaviour by changing one to affect the others. Neuroscience is now giving greater insight into how the brain changes structure when we learn/experience new things (Hanson, 2013).

Learning Points

What we tell ourselves – our internal script – affects how we feel and behave. These are just thoughts, but our brains believe what we tell them.

We can change the structure of our own brains by developing new ways of thinking and behaving. Reinforcing positive neural pathways helps them grow and replace negative ones.

References

Hanson, R. (2013). *Hardwiring Happiness: The Practical Science of Reshaping Your Brain and Your Life*. Ebury Publishing.
Seligman, M. (2011). *Flourish: A New Understanding of Happiness and Well-being*. Nicholas Beardsley.

DOI:10.4324/9781003180364-5

Script

Resources

YouTube video:
www.youtube.com/watch?v=Y71wViNy6wQ
"Unhelpful Thoughts."

Main learning points of the video:
- Explaining and demonstrating ways of thinking that make us feel worse
- Understanding we can change our thoughts
- Identifying the connection between thoughts, feelings, and behaviour

Icebreaker

Paper and pencil for each student

Handouts:

5.1   Alternative Explanations
5.2   Hot Seat Exercise
5.3   Real Life Practice

Purpose and Resources Required	*Plan*
Introduction	
Welcome	Welcome students, especially any who have returned after missing some sessions. Explain that although the sessions do follow on from each other, each session has something helpful to offer on its own. Reassure students that they are always welcome.
Review	
Session 5 Content	
	In our last session, we discussed our emotions and how important they are.
	What does anyone remember from the last session?
	How did you get on with your practice task? You were asked to draw and/or write about your calm place and notice your emotions when you were there.
	Share and discuss.
	So far, we have considered our physical reactions and our emotions when we are anxious. Today, we are going to look at our thoughts and see how they affect us.
	Remind students of the four aspects of the model if necessary.
Icebreaker	
Thinking About Who We Are	Give everyone a piece of paper and a pencil and allow five minutes for them to draw a picture that conveys who they are without writing any words or numbers. At the end of five minutes, the facilitator collects the pictures. Show the pictures to the group, one at a time, and have them try to guess who drew it. This can be one picture or a series of pictures, abstract or concrete; it is the student's choice.
Hand out paper and pencils if necessary.	
	Each student can then explain how their work expresses who they are.

Purpose and Resources Required	Plan
Teaching and Discussion	*A major factor in how we think is the way we interpret what is going on around us, the story we tell ourselves. Whenever something happens, we have control over the stories we tell ourselves, even if it doesn't feel like it at the time.*
	For example: entering a crowded room, our thoughts could be "I hate this. I will make a fool of myself; everyone will ignore me."
	Alternatively, we could think, "This will be fun. I am looking forward to meeting new people; my friends are here, and that makes me feel good."
	Which of those scenarios do you think would make us feel better/worse?
	Allow discussion.
Activity Video: "Unhelpful Thoughts"	Show video: https://www.youtube.com/watch?v=Y71wViNy6wQ "Unhelpful Thoughts"
	Have you ever felt like that? Do you call yourself names, tell yourself you are a "loser"? Are you being mean to yourself? Could you speak more kindly to yourself, the way a kind friend would speak? Could you look for more helpful thoughts? How did changing her thoughts change the way the girl in the video acted at the end?
	Discuss issues arising from the video; relate the issues to home and school/college/work.
Teaching	*The way we think affects the activity in our brains.*
	Science has shown that the more we think a certain thought, the more likely we are to think it again. This is due to neural wiring in the brain. It is a little like drawing a line in the sand and doing it many times until it has become very deep and entrenched.
	What is also interesting is that our brains believe what we tell them. So if we say, "I am rubbish" often enough, it becomes our go-to way of thinking and part of who we think we are.
Activity Handout 5.1: Alternative Explanations Looking at Alternative Perspectives	The following exercise can be done entirely orally if the group responds well to that approach. Handout 5.1 can be used as a consolidation exercise for individual work if the group is less amenable to discussion.
	I am going to read out some situations, and I want us all to think of all the unhelpful thoughts we could have, then some more helpful thoughts.
	One possibility would be to act out the scenarios with a student, briefly, and then discuss what thoughts the student may be having. Come up together with possible more helpful thoughts.
	First situation: *Your teacher/supervisor does not listen when you are telling them why you are late. What unhelpful things might you think?*
	Prompts, if necessary: "They don't care about me"; "They don't believe me."
	What would be more helpful thoughts?
	If necessary, prompt with "She's having a bad day"; "He is really keen to get on with the lesson"; "I can explain at break when she's not so busy."
	How might this change your feelings and behaviour?
	Second situation: *You are not picked for a part in a play/football team/choir. What unhelpful thoughts might you think?*
	Prompts if necessary: "I am a loser"; "It's not fair; they picked . . ."; "I will never be any good."
	Repeat with other suitable scenarios e.g., "Your mother is angry when you get home late."

Purpose and Resources Required	*Plan*
	If the group is comfortable together and willing to share, this activity can be repeated with real examples from within the group.
	Handout 5.2 can be used as a consolidation exercise if the group is less comfortable with discussion.
Activity Hot Seat Handout 5.2: Hot Seat Exercise	*The last activity showed us that changing our thoughts can change the way we feel and act. We are now going to apply that to ourselves.*
	We are going to take it in turns to be in the "hot seat" at the front of the group, The person in the hot seat will describe something that upset them: e.g., "Lucy ignored me in class today; I think she hates me!"
	It is the job of the rest of us to come up with more helpful thoughts, such as:
	"Maybe she was feeling unwell."
	"Perhaps she was struggling with the lesson you were in."
	"Maybe she is having a bad time at home and is feeling sad and depressed."
	"Maybe she thinks you don't want to be friends with her and needs reassurance from you."
	Record the responses.
	Facilitator now asks the student who has the problem:
	Which one of those do you think could be what's going on for Lucy?
	Now you have thought about that, how do you feel, and what do you think you will do next?
	Have your emotions and actions changed from the beginning?
	Ask others to take a turn in the hot seat and choose alternative scenarios: if possible, ones that are really going on in the students' lives.
Conclusion	*We can now see that changing our thoughts can change our emotions and behaviours.*
Practice Task Handout 5.3: Real Life Practice	*For our practice this week, I would like you all to use what we learnt today about thinking more helpful thoughts in a real situation. I am giving you a handout to record any event that happens this week. In the first column, put thoughts that are unhelpful and in the second, thoughts that are helpful in feeling and doing better.*
	Distribute Handout 5.3

Purpose and Resources Required	*Plan*

Relaxation Exercise

Five Senses

It is easy to think about the past ("Why did I . . .?") or the future ("What if I . . .?").

When we do that, we are focusing on events we cannot control, some over and some that have not yet happened. As we have learnt today, what we can control are our thoughts in the here and now.

Our relaxation exercise today will help us to focus on now.

Complete the "Five Senses" grounding exercise:

Look around you and notice:

- *Five things you can see*
- *Four things you can feel/touch*
- *Three things you can hear*
- *Two things you can smell*
- *One thing you can taste*

How was that? It is a helpful exercise to bring us "back to earth" or reality when we are "up in the air" or lost in imagining or thinking unpleasant thoughts. It is something you can try during the week and see if it calms you if you need it.

Allow three to five minutes for this relaxation exercise.

Thank you for today. I look forward to seeing you all at the next session.

5.1 Alternative Explanations

What happened:

1. Your supervisor does not listen when you are telling them why you are late.

2. Your mother/partner is angry when you are late home.

3. You fail an audition/try-out/interview.

Unhelpful Thoughts	Helpful Thoughts

5.2 Hot Seat Exercise

In the box, write something that happened to you that made you upset/anxious. Then write down some of the thoughts you had under Unhelpful Thoughts. Use your experience from the previous activity to find new ways of thinking about what happened.

What happened?

Unhelpful Thoughts	Hot Seat Thoughts

5.3 Real Life Practice

If something upsets you this week, write what it is that makes you upset/anxious. Then write down some of the thoughts you have under "Unhelpful Thoughts." Now think about those thoughts and see if you can come up with more "Helpful Thoughts" and write those in the next column.

What happened?

Unhelpful Thoughts	Helpful Thoughts

Session 6 Mindfulness

Facilitator Notes

Session Aims

Students are introduced to the concept of mindfulness in this session, and they are taught that there are simple mindfulness practices, such as "living in the moment," that can be adopted to help improve their lives. Students are given the opportunity to measure how mindful they are using our questionnaire. They are introduced to the concept of meditation and directed towards suitable resources if they are interested in learning more.

Theory

Mindfulness is a way of paying attention that originated in Eastern meditation practices. It has been described as "bringing one's complete attention to the present experience on a moment-to-moment basis" (Marlatt & Kristeller, 1999). It is understood that the mind requires training, usually through meditation, to achieve this. There is a growing body of evidence that mindfulness-based interventions can be effective with children and adolescents as well as adults (Dunning, L., 2018).

Learning Points

Anxiety can be over-concern with the future, and depression can be over-concern with the past. One way of combatting both is to develop a "mindful" approach to life, which allows us to experience fully the present moment without anxiety or depression interfering. There are simple techniques and practices that can assist us in this. Whilst these can only be touched on in one session, a few simple strategies can be easily learnt. A deeper understanding and experience would require further study.

References

Dunning, L., Griffiths, K., Kuyken, W., Crane, C., Foulkes, L., and Parker, J. (2018). The Effects of Mindfulness-Based Interventions on Cognition and Mental Health in Children and Adolescents – A Meta-Analysis of Randomized Controlled Trials. Journal of Child Psychology and Psychiatry. 60(3): 244–258.

Marlatt, G. A., and Kristeller, J. L. (1999). *Mindfulness and Meditation*. Available at: psycnet.apa.org

DOI:10.4324/9781003180364-6

Script

> ## Resources
>
> YouTube videos:
> www.youtube.com/watch?v=uUjDxAISCIQ
> "One-Minute Meditation"
>
> https://www.youtube.com/watch?v=WKwDyDtMnGQ
> "Three-Minute Mindful Breathing"
>
> Main learning points of the video:
> - This is a practical session and is used to introduce students to the concept of mindfulness.
> - The focus is on being in the present.
> - There are a range of other videos with scripts available on YouTube. Keep it short and simple at this stage.
>
> If the optional exercise is to be completed: one raisin/similar per person.
>
> There are many scripts for this exercise. One that we like can be found at https://ggie.berkeley.edu/practice/eating-a-raisin-with-mindfulness/#tab__2.
>
> ## Handouts
>
> 6.1 Mindfulness Questionnaire
> 6.2 Mindfulness Practice (You may also want to send this to students by email, so they have easy access to the links.)

Purpose and Resources Required	*Plan*
Introduction	
Welcome	Give a general welcome and remind the students that they are over halfway
Review	through the course of ten sessions.
	Last session we considered how changing the way we thought about a situation
	could also change our emotions and our behaviours.
	Discuss the practice task given last week. Ask if anyone used the five senses technique shared, and if so, how did it go?
Icebreaker	
Two Truths and a Lie (no resources required)	*We are now going to play a game called "Two Truths and a Lie." We each give three "facts" about ourselves, of which two are true, and one is not. The rest of the group must guess which one is the lie.*
	If the students are not familiar with the game, you might choose to go first, giving "facts" suitable to the age group of students. An example might be:
	"I have lived in six countries, been married twice, and have two children. One of those statements is not true. Now, you all guess which one of those statements is a lie."
	Who would like to go next?
	Give everyone an opportunity but allow students to pass.

Purpose and Resources Required	*Plan*
Session 6 Content	Remind students of the four-part model: physiology, emotions, thoughts, and behaviours.
	We have looked at how our physiology changes when we are anxious and what might happen to our thoughts and our emotions. In this session, we will look at ways we can change our physiology to enable us to think and behave more positively using "mindfulness" techniques.
Activity	
Video "One-Minute Meditation"	*We are going to start with a very brief introduction to meditation and mindfulness. Sit comfortably with your feet on the ground, eyes closed and get ready to do this very short meditation.*
	Play video:
	https://www.youtube.com/watch?v=uUjDxAISCIQ
	"One-Minute Meditation"
	Remind students of other relaxation techniques we have learnt
	over the first five sessions:
	• Diaphragmatic breathing
	• Square breathing
	• Five-minute de-stress activity
	• Calm place
	• Being in the present: five senses
	Discuss preferences and what works for whom.
	Remind the students that nothing works for everyone.
Teaching	*Today's meditation exercise helps us relax, start the day, or begin a specific task. Have you ever eaten a piece of cake or a treat without noticing you are eating it and then felt like you didn't really eat it? Or had a shower in which you were thinking so much about what you were going to do in the day that you were hardly aware you were showering? Mindfulness is about making sure we don't miss out on pleasurable experiences by staying in the moment and not living in the past or future. Depression involves spending too much time obsessing over the past; anxiety can be a type of obsessing about the future. There is a saying: "Yesterday is history; tomorrow is a mystery; today is a gift; that's why we call it the present."*
	Mindfulness comes originally from Eastern religious practices, although lots of religions have elements of meditation in them. Some mindfulness practices have been adopted by the positive psychology movement and many therapies, and there is a good evidence base that they work well for many people in combatting stress, depression, and anxiety. The one-minute meditation we started with was one such exercise. Of course, to benefit from these practices, they need repetition as your mind needs to be trained.

Purpose and Resources Required	*Plan*
Activity Handout 6.1: Mindfulness Questionnaire	*Academics have started to try to measure mindfulness, and there are several scales available to help people measure how mindful they are. Here is one that we have put together.* Distribute Handout 6.1. *Take a moment to fill one in for yourself. You won't have to share it, and you can score it later.* *You will notice that questions 2 and 9 are scored in the opposite way from the others. This is because those habits are unhelpful for mindfulness.*
Discussion	*What do you think of the questions? Do you see any areas you would like to work on for yourself? If so, you can mark those and score yourself again in a week or two when you have worked on them.*
Optional Activity Video or Script: Mindful Eating	Complete the exercise: mindfully eating a raisin. The facilitator can either play the video to the students or watch it earlier and take the students through the exercise without the video. https://ggie.berkeley.edu/practice/eating-a-raisin-with-mindfulness/#tab__2.
Conclusion	*In one session, we only have time to introduce the concept of mindfulness. It sounds easy to "live in the moment," but it can be very hard to do, and it takes practice to do it. Mindfulness also includes other concepts such as being non-judgmental of ourselves. If you find these ideas attractive to you, you can find more information on the internet.* *The importance of these practices is that they help us reduce the effect of the emotional parts of our brains (remember hijacking?!) and increase the probability that we will think more clearly using our frontal cortex.* *They also help us accept who we are and be less judgmental of ourselves.*
Relaxation Exercise "Three-Minute Mindful Breathing"	Play video: https://www.youtube.com/watch?v=WKwDyDtMnGQ "Three-Minute Mindful Breathing" Or choose one from Handout 6.2: Mindfulness Practice that you prefer. Keep it short: three to five minutes. *How do you feel now? It should help you feel relaxed and alert. Of course, this was just a taster; usually beginners are asked to start with ten-minute sessions and expand as they get more used to it. See how you get on with your practices during the week.*
Practice Task Handout 6.2: Mindfulness Practice	*For practice this week, I would like you try a mindfulness exercise to see if it helps you. Use one type of meditation/mindfulness activity once a day.* *You may choose to:* • *Replay the videos we have seen today.* • *Do one activity mindfully: e.g. eating, showering, listening.* • *Find alternative meditation relaxation videos from the practice sheet which I am giving out now.* Provide Handout 6.2 *Thanks for coming. Have a good week!*

6.1 Mindfulness Questionnaire

For each item, circle the number under the column that best applies to you (Rarely/Sometimes/Usually).

	Item	Rarely	Sometimes	Usually
1	I am good at noticing what is going on in the present moment.	1	2	3
2	I need to control everything. (Reverse Score)	3	2	1
3	I am able to concentrate well on things I find interesting.	1	2	3
4	I like spending time in nature.	1	2	3
5	I am good at giving myself time to relax.	1	2	3
6	I accept my thoughts and feelings even when I don't like them.	1	2	3
7	I try not to judge myself.	1	2	3
8	I practise self-compassion.	1	2	3
9	I spend a lot of time thinking about the past and the future. (Reverse Score)	3	2	1
10	I am good at noticing my feelings.	1	2	3

Score your responses out of 30. Total score...................... Date....................

The higher the score, the more mindful you are being. You might like to come back to this after you have worked on mindfulness for a while and see if anything has changed.

6.2 Mindfulness Practice

Choose one of the mindfulness meditations to practice. If you choose the one-minute meditation, use it at least daily.

"Mindful Breathing" (excellent three-minute relaxation)
https://www.youtube.com/watch?v=WKwDyDtMnGQ

One-minute relaxation with music (female, American voice)
www.youtube.com/watch?v=uUjDxAISCIQ

One minute (male, British voice)
www.youtube.com/watch?v=c1Ndym-IsQg

Additionally, you might like to try the 30-minute body scan at
www.dummies.com/religion/spirituality/the-mindfulness-body-scan/

Session 7 Facing Our Fears

Facilitator Notes

Session Aims

This session aims to help students understand that some behaviours maintain feelings of fear and anxiety. Avoiding experiences that make us anxious, for example, may give short-term relief but maintains and/or increases feelings of fear and anxiety in the long term. The cycle of avoidant behaviour and its consequences will be discussed.

Where situations currently being avoided are safe and beneficial, we encourage students to "feel the fear and do it anyway." Although the feelings may be uncomfortable, they are not dangerous.

In this session, we will start to find ways to work towards new behaviours which allow us to face our fears and not avoid them.

Theory

Behavioural science tells us that avoidance leads to increased anxiety; trying out new behaviours allows anxiety to reduce and our skills to grow (Stallard, 2014). This has led to exposure therapy, which involves exposing a person to their fears gradually whilst being supported, in a good frame of mind, and in a safe environment emotionally.

Acceptance and commitment therapy (Hayes, 2019) is helpful in recognising that some unpleasant thoughts and feelings are inevitable, and it is important to manage them rather than avoid them.

Learning Points

Exposing ourselves to fear in a controlled, safe environment moves us forward, whereas avoidance maintains anxiety. If we do not face up to our fears, we won't get rid of the anxiety; we only escape it temporarily, and we limit our lives. Accepting our feelings and thoughts and working with them can reduce our stress and help us move forward more easily. It is helpful to try out new behaviours in small steps to start facing our fears. Changing our behaviours can help us change thoughts and feelings and so help us towards a more fulfilled and exciting life.

References

Hayes, S. (2019). *A Liberated Mind*. Penguin Random House.
Stallard, P. (2014). *Think Good Feel Good*. Wiley.

DOI:10.4324/9781003180364-7

Script

Resources

YouTube video:
www.youtube.com/watch?v=-CAd9o9OlqM
"Anxiety/Avoidance Cycle"

Main learning points of the video:
- Anxiety increases over time when we avoid situations.
- The costs of short–term relief.
- Breaking the cycle of anxiety.

Handouts

7.1   Unhelpful Behaviours
7.2   Avoidance Cycle
7.3   Small Steps to Goal
7.4   Guided Visualisation

Guided visualisation: only one required for the facilitator during the session, but students may wish to take away a written or recorded version.

Purpose and Resources Required	*Plan*

Introduction

Welcome	Welcome students, noticing if any have returned after missing a session or two.
Review	
Session 7 Content	*Last session, we looked at mindfulness and whether it could help us reduce our feelings of stress and make better decisions.*
	How did the practice task go?
	Discuss preferences, methods, advantages, and disadvantages of different approaches.

Teaching

Comfort Zones	*Today we are looking at our behaviours and seeing which of them make us less likely to be anxious and stressed and which we can choose to help us feel better over time.*
	We all have our own comfort zone. Everything in our comfort zone feels completely normal. However, when things outside our comfort zone are new, uncertain, or scary, our bodies try to warn us by activating the anxiety alarm. From an evolutionary perspective, we are "hard wired" to try and avoid pain, including emotional discomfort, as we saw in Session 1.
	However, the hard wiring is to protect us from physical pain and maintain our survival. We still have the same mechanisms working in our brains, but we are now usually responding to perceived, future pain: e.g., the anxiety of going into a new social situation or taking an exam. Being outside our comfort zone leads to "What if?" questions as discussed in Session 5.

Activity	*Think of the last time you felt anxious and note down some of your "What if?" thoughts: e.g., What if I make a fool of myself? What if no one speaks to me? What if I can't do it?*
	Discuss in pairs.

Purpose and Resources Required	Plan

Teaching
Share with the group.

Getting comfortable doing something that is currently outside our comfort zone needs effort and practice. The closer we get to new or frightening things, the greater the anxiety grows and the harder it gets to do.

However, developing and growing as a person involves trying things that are outside our comfort zone: e.g., riding a bike, learning to swim, going to interviews, making presentations, meeting new people. Without this, our lives become very limited and restricted and not much fun at all.

Clearly, sometimes our anxiety is accurate when it is warning us not to do something dangerous. However, it is often, by mistake, telling us not to do something that is quite safe.

It is important that when we feel that sort of anxiety in our bodies, we recognise it for what it is – i.e., a false alarm – and accept that it is there but move towards the action we are anxious about. If we avoid a situation when we are anxious, although it relieves the emotional discomfort in the short term, in the long term, it will increase anxiety as it becomes our default behaviour.

Remember the stress bucket? Avoiding something we fear increases the amount of stress that will fall into our buckets.

We tend to repeat the behaviours and thoughts we are used to having as the connections in our brains get reinforced.

Discussion
Handout 7.1:
Unhelpful Behaviours

There are several strategies we tend to use that give us short-term relief from the difficult feelings that go with anxiety and fear.

Provide Handout 7.1: Unhelpful Behaviours.

These are behaviours that maintain or increase our anxiety levels.

Discuss examples of the behaviours we use sometimes that might fall into these categories.

Ask students to write in any examples that they or others use at times.

Activity
Handout 7.2:
Avoidance Cycle
Video: "Anxiety Cycle"

Today we are going to concentrate on just one of these behaviours: avoidance.

Provide Handout 7.2: Avoidance Cycle

Play the video:

https://www.youtube.com/watch?v=-CAd9o9OlqM

"Anxiety Cycle"

Discuss in groups of two or three.

Are you aware of avoiding situations you don't find easy?

What are they?

Does this work for you in the short term?

Does this work for you in the long term?

Purpose and Resources Required	*Plan*
Teaching Handout 7.3: Small Steps to Goal.	*Sometimes it is important to break a new activity into small steps and try to achieve one at a time, before going for the total behaviour.* *For example:* *Adam wants to go karting with his friends. However, to get there, he has to go on a train. He finds going on public transport frightening, although he doesn't really know why. He also finds going to new places difficult, especially if he must go alone. He knows that staying at home whilst his friends have fun will make him feel sad and left out.* *How could this be broken down into small steps which Adam would feel he could handle?* *Example:* 1. *Walk to the station and find out times of trains and cost of a ticket.* 2. *Meet a friend at the station and buy tickets ahead of the journey.* 3. *Try out the train journey with a friend and plan the route to the karting track from the station.* 4. *Plan a date for a karting trip with others.* 5. *Plan a clear time and meeting place for the whole group.* Provide Handout 7.3: Small Steps to Goal. *Choose something you find difficult and break it down into small steps.* *Each step should feel manageable, and if it does not, it needs to be broken down further.*
Conclusion	*Here are the main points from today:* *There are several behaviours that we use to help us avoid short-term emotional discomfort.* *We call these "maintenance behaviours."* *We have looked in detail at how avoidance behaviours might give short-term relief but lead to a lack of new learning and trying new and fun activities.* *Facing our fears, although not easy, can help reduce our anxiety and help us realise we can do new things and lead a more fulfilled and interesting life.* *Breaking new and difficult tasks into small steps is one way of accomplishing them.*
Practice Task	*This week, I would like you to try out the first step (or two) on your plan.* *Does this feel like something you can have a go at?* *When would be a good time for you to try out this task?* *Would it be helpful to do it with someone or easier on your own?* *Alternatively, keep a daily tally of the number of times you notice that you are using any of the behaviours that maintain anxiety.* Record this on paper or on your phone.

Purpose and Resources Required	*Plan*
Relaxation Exercise Handout 7.4: Guided Visualisation	*Let's begin with a few deep breaths: in through the nose (notice your belly expanding), out slowly through your mouth. We will do this three times.* *Now close your eyes or focus on a point in the distance whilst I take you through a relaxing guided visualisation.* Read the Guided Visualisation script, slowly and calmly. When finished, ask students to feel the floor with their feet, feel their arms on the desk, and open their eyes to make sure they are back in the present. *What are you all going to do after this session?* *Thank you for participating today. Look forward to seeing you next time.*

7.1 Unhelpful Behaviours

When we are feeling anxious, we naturally do things that make us feel better. Some of the things we do only make us feel better in the short term but, in the longer term, can make things worse. By doing the following things, we unintentionally maintain our anxiety:

Avoidance

We can temporarily reduce unpleasant feelings by avoiding taking part in the feared activity (e.g., not going on public transport, dropping out of sporting activities, not taking exams or tests).

Superstitions/Obsessions

We may develop behaviours, such as rituals and habits which give a false sense of security, in the mistaken belief that they will keep us safe (e.g., not walking on cracked paving stones or repeating actions unnecessarily). Or we may do unhealthy things like hair pulling, nail biting, or over- or under-eating, which may give temporary relief but hurt us in time.

Talking Unkindly to Ourselves

It is easy to be hard on ourselves. We call ourselves "stupid" or "cowardly." We may "catastrophise"—leap from one minor event to imagining that disaster is now inevitable (e.g., "I stumbled over some words in a presentation, now everyone will think I am stupid. I will never pass this course, then I won't get a decent job, and my life will be ruined!").

Mind Reading

This is assuming that we know what is going on in the other person's head and believing it to be a true fact. This becomes a problem, if we believe they are having negative thoughts about us, e.g., "That person is thinking that I look stupid"; "She doesn't like me"; "He is cross with me."

Hypervigilance

When we are anxious, we watch for danger and treat many situations as potentially threatening even if they are not. We are overly alert, looking for danger in benign things, interpreting every sound as a threat, every negative facial expression as directed at ourselves, all events as risks.

In My Case, I

....

....

....

7.2 Avoidance Cycle

7.3 Small Steps to Goal

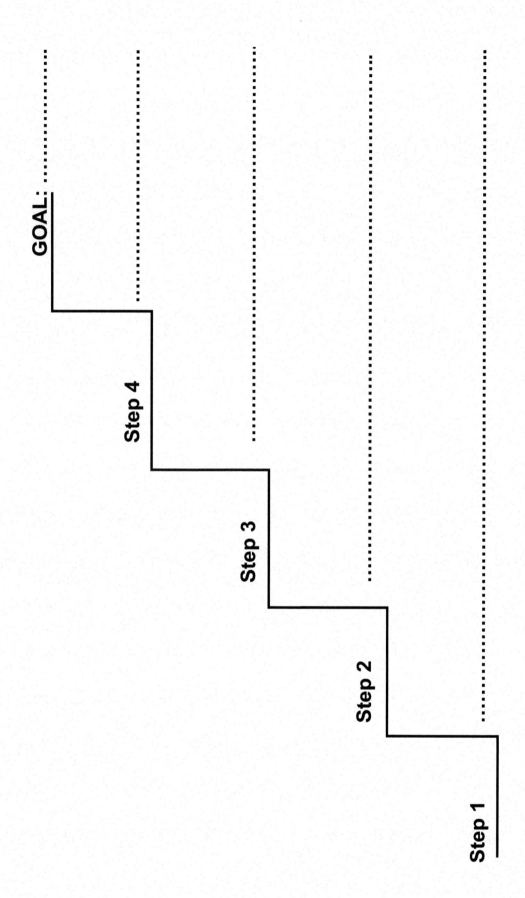

7.4 Guided Visualisation

> **Relaxing can be difficult sometimes. The following exercise is a guided relaxation script which can help relieve stress and anxiety.**
>
> **The script can be read to a person or group, and/or it can be recorded so that it can be played back whenever it is needed.**
>
> **If you wish, you can play relaxing music whilst reading this to the person/group.**

Script

First, make yourself comfortable; you can sit or lie down. (ALLOW GROUP TO FIND COMFORTABLE POSITIONS.)

Gently close your eyes, and slowly breathe in and out through your nose. (PAUSE.) Take in a deep breath, and slowly let it out. (PAUSE.) Take in another deep breath, and slowly breathe out. (PAUSE.)

Imagine you are walking in a garden on a pleasantly warm day. (PAUSE.) On a bench sits a friendly looking woman in brightly coloured, strange-looking clothes. She is sewing and has a basket of brightly coloured materials by her side. (PAUSE.) She tells you that this is the garden of tranquillity. (PAUSE.) While you are there, you can leave all your worries with her, and she will stitch them into a quilt. (PAUSE.) You leave all your worries with her and walk on. (PAUSE.)

There is lush, green grass with flowers scattered everywhere. (PAUSE.) You lie down on it. (PAUSE). You look up into the beautiful blue sky. (PAUSE.) You see white fluffy clouds like cotton tufts. (PAUSE.) You watch as a big soft cloud gently drifts towards you. (PAUSE.) See it float gently down to the ground. Climb onto the cloud. (PAUSE.) Feel how soft and comfortable it is. As you breathe, feel the softness of the cloud. (PAUSE.) You notice that the cloud is turning pink. As you breathe in, you fill your lungs with the lovely soft, calm pink of the cloud. (PAUSE.) Enjoy the calm feeling. (PAUSE.) Think of your favourite colour. As you think of it, the cloud slowly changes to that colour. (PAUSE.) Take a deep breath, and breathe in your favourite colour. Breathe in and out slowly. (PAUSE.) Change the colour of the cloud. Notice how that colour feels. (PAUSE.) Change the colour one more time. Notice how that colour feels. (PAUSE.) Now, as you breathe out, watch all the colours flow out of the cloud like a rainbow.

(PAUSE.) Say to yourself, "I am relaxed. I feel good. The colours are pretty and relaxing." (PAUSE.) Take another breath, and blow the rainbow cloud away. Watch it drift back up into the sky. (PAUSE.) You are back lying on the lush grass. (PAUSE.)

You get up and walk back the way you came. (PAUSE.) You meet the sewing lady who has sewn all your worries into a slightly odd, brightly coloured quilt. (PAUSE.) She lets you choose whether you want to take it with you or leave it with her. (PAUSE.) You walk back out of the tranquil garden. (PAUSE.)

When you are ready, wiggle your fingers and toes. Open your eyes and stretch. Notice how relaxed and good you feel.

This has been adapted from:

"50 Activities for Teaching Emotional Intelligence. Level 1 Elementary" Publ. PRO-ED 1996, Introduction and Theory by Dianne Schilling.

and also

Go-Zen

Many more relaxation scripts can be found on YouTube.

Session 8 Lifestyle

Facilitator Notes

Session Aims

In this session, we will consider the importance of the link between our bodies and our minds. Our mental health and our physical health have profound effects on each other.

By changing our physical health, we can change our mental health and reduce anxiety. Small changes to our lifestyle can make a big difference to our mental health. The aim is to encourage students to assess their own lifestyles and consider how changes could be made. Students have the opportunity to take on a "coaching" role to help one another consider small changes they can make.

Theory

The mind and body are inextricably linked (Maslow, 1968). A healthy body assists tremendously in having a happy, healthy mind. As young people mature, they are in the in-between stage when they have increasing, but still limited, power over their lifestyle. If they have formed unhealthy habits, they will need sensitive help to change. This session introduces the idea that even teenagers can start to take control of some aspects of their lifestyle (Day, J.). Contributing to society is also a necessary part of a meaningful, fulfilling life (Seligman, 2017). Social media is touched on as a new but hugely important part of a young person's experience.

Learning Points

Whilst we cannot change everything in our lives, there are some things we can change. Ten lifestyle areas are discussed, all of which have a profound effect on mental health. Change is difficult, but with motivation and support, we can improve our lives. A coaching method is used to encourage the students to assist one another, and they are given suitable questions to ask. This type of questioning may be helpful when thinking through difficult issues alone or with a friend.

References

Day, J. The Art of Emotion [YouTube Channel]. "Emotion Revolution, Tips to Help Manage Your Emotions." Available at: www.Youtube.com/EmotionRevolution

Maslow, A. H. (1968). *Towards a Psychology of Being.* Van Nostrand.

Seligman, M. (2017). *Authentic Happiness: Using the New Positive Psychology to Realise Your Potential for Lasting Fulfilment.* Nicholas Brealy Publishing.

DOI:10.4324/9781003180364-8

Script

Resources

YouTube videos
https://www.youtube.com/watch?v=_HEnohs6yYw
"The Choice" (short animated movie)

Main learning points from the video:
- We make small choices at many points in the day.
- Small choices turn into habits.
- Habits become a way of life.
- Making small changes can make a big difference.

www.youtube.com/watch?v=kWICigGOptw
"Boost your Immune System"

Main learning points from the video:
- Relaxation can boost our immune system.
- Gives students the experience a brief meditation.

An alternative to using video would be for the facilitator to choose a meditation, of which there are many on YouTube, and read it to the students.

Handouts

8.1   What Is a Healthy Lifestyle?
8.2   The Wheel of Life
8.3   Lifestyle Coaching Notes

Optional: Rugs/mats for use with relaxation if students choose to lie down.

Purpose and Resources Required	*Plan*
Introduction	
Welcome	Welcome the group back and appreciate the tenacity of those who are sticking with the course.
Review	
Session 8 Content	*In the last session, we considered facing our fears and changing our behaviours. How did you manage with the last practice session? You were asked to look at identifying some small steps towards new behaviours and trying them out. How did you get on?*
Video: "The Choice"	
	Allow discussion.
	Did you find the guided visualisation from last session helpful? Has anyone used it this week?
	Allow discussion.
	Today, we are going to consider our lifestyles and how they may or may not help us with feeling good.
	This may sound difficult to do, but there is a great deal of research that tells us that small changes to our lifestyles can make a big difference to our sense of well-being.
	Show video:
	https://www.youtube.com/watch?v=_HEnohs6yYw
	"The Choice"

Purpose and Resources Required	*Plan*
Teaching The importance of making healthy lifestyle choices Small changes over time make a big difference. What is a healthy lifestyle?	*As we mature, we gain more control over our lives. As young people, you may have less control over your lives than most adults, but control is increasing all the time. If you think about when you were seven years old and now, what decisions do you make in your life now that you did not make then?* Allow discussion. *Anxiety is affected by what is going on in our lives. Remember the bucket analogy in Session 2? We all have a certain size bucket for containing stress, and some strategies we use fill the bucket; some allow it to empty.* *Today, we are looking at the background to anxiety in our lives and looking for things we can change to improve our mental and physical health. We are going to think about ten aspects of lifestyle. I want you to be thinking about yourself and anything you could improve in your own life. Afterwards, we will help each other think it through.* *The following are all well-researched aspects of a happy and healthy lifestyle. You may not have control over all areas of your life, but you each have some freedom to make a positive change. You just need to find it and act on it. Small changes can make a big difference.*
Discussion Handout 8.1: What Is a Healthy Lifestyle? Identify areas of lifestyle to which students relate well.	Provide Handout 8.1: What Is a Healthy Lifestyle? Take the students through it or allow them time to read and discuss it.
Activity Handout 8.2: The Wheel of Life This activity helps students visualise a balanced lifestyle as opposed to an unbalanced lifestyle. Handout 8.3: Life Coaching Notes Peer group support to make changes	*Imagine a bicycle: one with unbalanced wheels would be wobbly, and tiny wheels are less stable than large ones. To work well, bicycle wheels should be beautiful round circles. We are now going to look at how rounded our lives are.* Provide Handout 8.2: The Wheel of Life. *Take a few moments to rate each aspect of your lifestyle.* *Decide how you are doing on a scale of 1 to 10, where 1 is an extremely serious and urgent problem, and 10 is perfect.* *Once you have rated yourself, you can draw a line between the points marked to give a visual picture of how balanced your lifestyle is.* Allow the students time to rate themselves. *Now we are going to help each other think through our lifestyles. One person will be the life coach; another will be the client; the rest will be assistant coaches.* Depending on the size of the group, you can do this all together or split into smaller groups of two or three. Provide Handout 8.3: Life Coaching Notes. Ask the group to read it and answer any questions. Split the group into twos or threes. One is the client who shares their issue and the second is the coach who helps them explore it. If in threes, the third is the assistant coach who can make suggestions if the coach gets stuck. Ask for a volunteer to be the client and another the coach. Encourage the students to help each other find at least one positive change they can make. Based on the time available, encourage students to change roles where possible.

Purpose and Resources Required	Plan
Discussion Elicit one area of change that each student feels they can manage this week.	*How did you find that activity?* *Which areas seem the easiest to change and which the most difficult?*
Practice Task Make one small change to individual lifestyle.	*Did you all find at least one area you thought you could make a small change in?* *The practice task this week will be to make one change you have highlighted. Make a note on your Wheel of Life worksheet about what you will change and how.* *Be ready to tell everyone how it went next session. Make sure it is realistic and manageable for you.*
Conclusion Revisit and summarise the main learning points.	*Today, we considered the importance of the link between our bodies and our minds. Our mental health and our physical health have profound effects on each other.* *We looked at ways we can improve our health by making small changes to our lifestyle. Change is not easy, but with support, we can make improvements. Helping each other, as in our coaching session, can be very beneficial in helping us make and maintain changes.*
Relaxation Exercise Meditation Optional: Rugs/mats if there is space and students feel comfortable lying down Video: "Boost Your Immune System"	*Our relaxation today is a short meditation to help us boost our immune system. You can do it sitting comfortably, or if you would like (and there is space), you can listen to it lying down.* *Is everyone comfortable? OK, let's start.* Play video: https://www.youtube.com/watch?v=kWICigGOptw "Boost Your Immune System" *Any questions about this session?* *Have a great week everyone. I look forward to seeing you at our next session and hearing how you got on with changing something in your lifestyle.*

8.1 What Is a Healthy Lifestyle?

Lifestyle Area	Aim
Exercise	I exercise regularly for one to two hours a day.
Diet	I eat plenty of fruit and vegetables; high fibre/whole-grain carbohydrates (potatoes, bread, rice, pasta); smaller quantities of beans, pulses, fish, eggs, and meat; and only a little of dairy products. I drink six to nine cups of water a day and only have minimal caffeine and high-sugar foods and drinks.
Sleep	I sleep for eight or nine hours a night.
Technology and social media	I spend less than two hours a day screen time, excluding work/homework. I always think before I respond. I don't get involved in online dramas. I don't get distressed by what I read online.
Self-worth	I accept myself and practice self-compassion, not being a perfectionist, recognising that mistakes show I am learning. I do not harm myself.
Spirituality/creativity	I take part in one or more of the following: prayer and/or meditation; spending time enjoying nature; creative activities such as art, drawing, poetry, singing, dancing, listening to music, etc.
Organisation	I am able to get my homework/chores completed on time, without staying up late, and without stress.
Relaxation	I have at least three separate strategies in place for relaxing when stress builds up: e.g., taking a walk, breathing exercises, phoning a friend, thinking helpful thoughts.
Alcohol, tobacco, and illegal drugs	I avoid these.
Community involvement	I have a regular commitment to one or more of the following: volunteering; post of responsibility; chores at home; caring for another person, pet, or plant.

8.2 The Wheel of Life

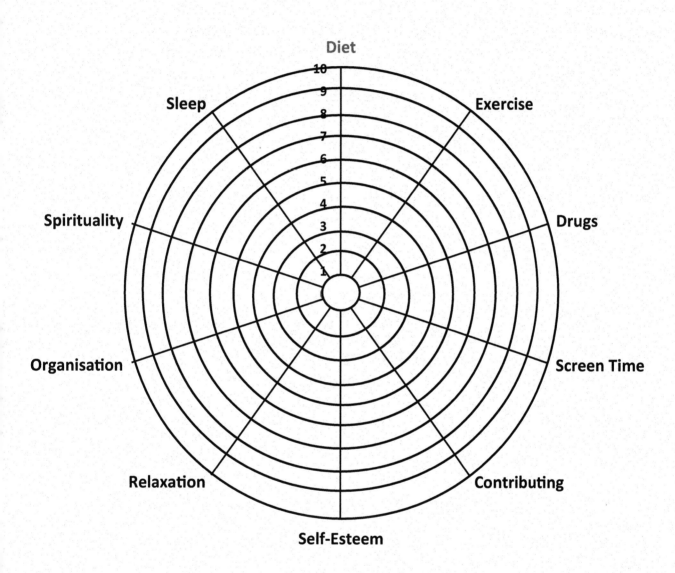

8.3 Lifestyle Coaching Notes

Group Work

To take place after everyone has rated their lifestyle on the Wheel of Life.

Where possible, enable everyone to have the chance of being client, coach, and assistant coach.

Notes for Client

The life coaches are here to help you work out how best to make changes to improve your life. You can choose to change one or two things (not too much at once). You might choose to change something easy to have a quick win, you might choose to change something that has shown up as a wobble on your wheel as it needs some change, or you might choose something difficult but that you are motivated to change. Remember, this is your life, so you decide.

Notes for Life Coach

Your job is to help your client think through and decide what they want to do. (You don't tell them). Try the following questions:

- Have you selected something you would like to work on to improve your life?
- What have you chosen, and why would you wish it to change?
- Have you thought about what you could do?
- What has worked for you before?
- What are the challenges that have stopped you so far?
- Can you see any ways around that?
- What are you going to commit to trying this week?

Notes for Assistant Coaches

Your job is to use your best listening skills to understand what the client wishes to change and what is getting in their way. If the coach gets stuck, you can help by asking helpful questions. Try to avoid saying things like "You should . . ." Instead say things like:

- Would it help if you . . . ?
- Have you ever tried . . . ?
- What has worked for me is . . .
- Could you think about it this way . . . ?

The outcome is to identify at least one area to change.

Session 9 Identifying Our Strengths

Facilitator Notes

Session Aims

The aims of this session are to recognise that, as human beings, we are predisposed to notice what is going badly rather than what is going well; this is called the "negativity bias." We also want students to understand that being good at something does not mean being perfect. A further aim is to reinforce that our abilities and skills are not fixed but can always improve with practice. This is called having a "growth mind set."

This will be the penultimate session of the course, and the students may need some help in preparing for the ending. This includes how they put in place the strategies they have learnt without a weekly group to motivate them. It may also include whether and how members of the group choose to maintain their relationships with each other. They may welcome a follow-up session organised by the facilitator a few weeks after the course has ended. This should be discussed with the students, and, if appropriate, a date planned.

Theory

Theories of cognitive neuroscience and evolutionary psychology have demonstrated the power of the negativity bias (Hanson, 2013).

Social learning takes place through observation of others. Mirror neurones have a powerful effect in shaping our behaviours and emotions when observing others (Murden, 2020). These neurones reflect others' thoughts and feelings, which helps us empathise but also makes us susceptible to being overly influenced by others' views and feelings.

Learning Points

We are biased to notice the negative aspects of our characters just as we were with perceptions of others' behaviours in Session 5.

Reflecting on what we are good at can help us become more resilient and improve our well-being.

Learning from others is an important part of our social development.

We are all unique and have different strengths.

References

Hanson, R. (2013). *Hardwiring Happiness: The Practical Science of Reshaping Your Brain and Your Life*. Ebury Publishing.
Murden, F. (2020). *Mirror Thinking: How Role Models Make Us Human*. Bloomsbury Stigma.

DOI:10.4324/9781003180364-9

Script

Resources

YouTube video
https://m.youtube.com/watch?v=3Aem-dluC80
"Strengths and Challenges"

Main learning points from the video:
- We all have different strengths and challenges.
- Identifying and working to our strengths helps us feel better.
- It is OK that some people are better at different things than we are.

Handouts

9.1   Prepared in advance: strength cards, printed and cut out into cards (two copies)
9.2   Aide Memoire for Reflection

Personal whiteboards/paper and pens

Optional: mobile phone(s)/camera for photographing strengths exercise

---

Purpose and Resources Required	*Plan*
Introduction Welcome Review Session 9 Content	By this stage, the facilitator will know the group well and can give a suitable welcome and motivate them for this session. It will be important to remind the students that this is the penultimate session of the course.
	Next week will be the last session of our course, and we have done a lot of work together. I will miss you all when we finish. It would be helpful to think about whether and how you wish to keep in touch with each other.
	Last week, we were trying to make one lifestyle change. Our coaches helped us make decisions about this. How did everyone get on?
	Take feedback from a group discussion.
	What have we learnt from the activity? Did you pick good goals? Did you have enough time or opportunity to try out your new plan? Do you want to continue with this or try something different?
	Did anyone use the relaxation we tried out last week or something else that we have explored over the sessions to help us relax?
	We only have one more session after this, and we have talked a great deal about what is difficult for us. So today, we are going to concentrate on what we are good at so that we appreciate our own special skills and how unique we all are.

Purpose and Resources Required	*Plan*

Teaching

The Negativity Bias	*We discussed earlier in the course how easy it is for us to think negatively. We are about three times as likely to notice what we have difficulties with than what we are good at. When we are with others, we may perceive their intentions towards us as more negative than positive.*
Recognising strengths in others is sometimes easier than in ourselves. We also need to identify our own strengths.	*A natural response to positive experiences has been called "Teflon" or non-stick as they slip off us very easily, sometimes without our even noticing them. Negative experiences have been described as "Velcro" or glue as they can stick with us for a very long time.*
Video: "Strengths and Challenges"	*If you have a good relationship with someone most of the time, you may find that one slip up when you either feel they hurt you or worry that you have hurt them may stand out more clearly than all the good memories.*
	This "negativity bias" was a useful attribute for us when we needed to protect ourselves physically. Imagine being on the grasslands as an early human being. The sun is shining, and everything is peaceful and quiet. Then you notice a twitch in the tall grass a hundred metres away. You have to be on immediate alert in case it is a lion or tiger, and your body reacts. Your bias towards looking for danger may save your life. Now, our bodies sometimes make the mistake of reacting like we are threatened by a lion when, in fact, we just have to go to a party or give a presentation. It is useful to have insight into our own weaknesses, too, but not at the cost of overlooking our strengths.
	When we can appreciate our own strengths and achievements, we become more confident, engaged, and better connected with others. This helps us improve our resilience and reduces anxiety and stress.
	Show video: https://m.youtube.com/watch?v=3Aem-dluC80
	"Strengths and Challenges"
	It can be hard to recognise our strengths — often, it's easier to see the strengths in others, so let's start here.
	Over the past few weeks, you have got to know each other as a group and will have noticed things that you like and respect about each other. We do not very often say what we appreciate about each other, so now is our chance to do that.

Purpose and Resources Required	*Plan*
Activity Handout 9.1: Strength Cards (pre-prepared) Optional: Mobile phone or camera to photograph strength cards chosen	On the table, place the prepared strength cards face up. Give the students the opportunity to look through the statements. Depending on the dynamics of the group, the facilitator might want to start with themself or one of the more confident members of the group. *We are going to take it in turns for the other members of the group to choose strengths that they think each of us has. Do we have a volunteer to go first? Thank you [student name]* *I am going to ask each of you to choose a card which describes a strength that you have seen in [student name].* To turn this into a game, the facilitator might ask the chosen student to turn their back so they can't see which cards are being selected until all have been chosen. When all have been chosen, *[student name]* can turn back to the group. *Now I would like each of you in turn to show [student name] the strength card you have chosen and tell them why.* If a student is keen to mention a strength not on a card, they can write their own on paper or their whiteboard to share. This is repeated by each person in the group. Give the student the opportunity to lay out their cards and take a photo of them to be able to refer to as an aide memoire. Remembering how they are positively perceived may give them a sense of pride. An optional extension to this activity would then be to ask each student to pick out two cards which they believe show the strengths that they perceive themselves to have and explain why. *How did you feel doing this activity? What was it easier to do: see the strengths in others or yourself? Why do you think that is? Which of your strengths do you think can help you when you are finding life difficult and how?* Allow discussion.
Teaching The importance of social observation to help us learn new skills and strategies.	*When we are in a social group, we have a natural propensity to feel what others in the group are feeling and to be drawn to behave as they do. This is because we have evolved as social animals; we are usually safer in a group and learn as much from each other as we do on our own.* *This is helpful but can also be problematic. It is why peer pressure is so powerful. In our brains, we have mirror neurones which help us reflect others' thoughts and feelings. It is easy to learn things that are not helpful or be pressured into behaving in ways we are not comfortable with. This is why it is important to choose our friends and role models with care.*
Activity Choose a personal role model. Personal whiteboards and markers/ pens and paper or 'phones.	*Sometimes, even knowing what your strengths are, you might still find some situations difficult. On such occasions, it is good to have a positive "go-to" person you admire and respect, someone who is calm and appears to do the right thing, a positive role model.* *Make a note on your whiteboard/paper/phone the name of one celebrity or person you know whose values align with your own and who you have respect and admiration for.* Allow thinking time. *So, the next time you are unsure what to do, stop, take a second and ask yourself what that person would do in the same situation.* *Let's think of some scenarios. For example, you are feeling anxious about going in for a test; you don't want to go in. What would your chosen role model do?*

Purpose and Resources Required	*Plan*
Conclusion	*We have seen today that it is all too easy to focus on the things we are not good at and what we feel we do not do well. Recognising and identifying our strengths can help us challenge our negative thoughts and find ways to solve problems.*
	Using others as role models is also a very good way to learn new skills and strategies.
Practice Task Handout 9.2: Aide Memoire for Reflection	*Next week will be our last session, and I will miss meeting with you! By the time we finish, I would like you all to have identified your own set of strategies and skills that you can use when you feel anxious and stressed.*
	You might like to choose a mixture of
	• *Short term (e.g., a relaxation technique)*
	• *Medium term (e.g., a behaviour change) and*
	• *Long term (e.g., a lifestyle change)*
	To help you do that, I am giving you an aide memoire of some of the things we have covered in this course. Before we meet for our next session, please read it through and use it to reflect on how helpful you have found these things. There is space for you to make your own notes of useful ideas, tips, and strategies in each area.
	Next week, we will use this to create our own action plan to take away with us after we have finished working together. I would like you to come prepared for that next time. I would also like to celebrate how hard you have all worked and how far you have all come.
	Depending on the time/venue/practicalities, the facilitator may wish to provide a cake and juice, or the whole group might wish to bring dishes for a shared meal to celebrate completing the course. This can be discussed and agreed here. Older students may wish to go out together as a group to celebrate.
Relaxation Exercise Starting to review relaxation exercises and developing group decision-making skills Reminders to students of what to bring next week	*This week, I would like us to choose a relaxation task you enjoyed from this course or if any of us have a favourite one they have discovered elsewhere and would like to share with the group. Which shall we do?*
	Allow discussion and complete the chosen exercise. The facilitator may wish to come with one prepared in case no one remembers a preference.
	Well done for making it so far. We are 90% of the way through our course. I look forward to seeing you next week at our last session. We will be looking at how far we have come, so please bring with you:
	• Your Personal Goals from Session 1
	• If you decided to follow up on mindfulness, your Mindfulness Questionnaire from Session 6
	• Your Aide Memoire from today, having thought about and noted what worked best for you
	Remind the students of the celebration agreed and what, if anything, they need to bring to eat or drink.
	I am really looking forward to seeing you all next week when we can celebrate all we have learnt.

9.1 Strength Cards

Prior to the session, copies of these should be printed and cut into individual cards.

I am creative

I can achieve my dreams

I am enthusiastic

I am a true friend

I respect myself

I am wise

I am beautiful

I am focused and determined

I am healthy and strong

I make friends easily

I am relaxed and calm

I forgive others easily

Good things come my way

I am courageous

I am in charge of my life

I am willing to try

I am strong and secure

I see the best in others

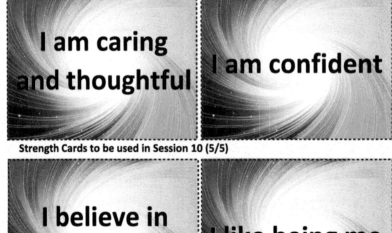

I am caring and thoughtful

I am confident

Strength Cards to be used in Session 10 (5/5)

I believe in myself

I like being me

I am strong

I am grateful

9.2 Aide Memoire for Self-Reflection

	Anxiety-Relieving Strategy	My Notes
Self-Analysis	**Self-Awareness** Notice when you experience an anxiety symptom, thought, or behaviour before it becomes unmanageable.	
	Physical Symptoms Notice and record your physical reactions when you are stressed.	
	The "Anxiety Alarm" Check if this is a real danger. If not, remind yourself that your amygdala "anxiety alarm" has gone off unnecessarily. This is just the fight/flight/freeze response.	
	Keep Grounded Recognise what is happening now – not what happened in the past or might happen in the future. Stay in the present. Notice five things you can see, four things you hear, three things you can touch, two things you can smell, and one thing you can taste.	
	Acceptance Remember that it's OK to feel afraid or worried – it's how you act to deal with it that's important.	
Relaxation	**Breathing Techniques** Take a slow, deep breath and let it out slowly. Or try one of the techniques learnt on the course: diaphragmatic/belly breathing or square breathing.	
	Muscle Relaxation Techniques Start with your eyes: clench, hold, and relax. Work down your body, clenching, holding, then releasing your muscle groups.	
	Listening Listen to a guided fantasy, meditation, or relaxation audio. Or, if you prefer, listen to your favourite music.	
	Thought Techniques Imagine your calm place. Use your calm thoughts, object or picture.	
	Drawing or Writing Draw or write about your calm place or a happy memory.	

	Anxiety-Relieving Strategy	My Notes
Challenge the Negative	**Stop Technique** When you feel your anxiety levels increasing, tell yourself to stop. Take a deep breath and think about what you need to do.	
	Alternative Perspectives Rethink the situation – can you change this from a negative thought to a positive thought?	
	Using a Role Model What would your role model do in the same situation? What would you advise someone else to do if they were in your situation?	
	Asking a Friend Share your feelings with someone you trust; don't bottle them up.	
Lifestyle	**Practicing Gratitude** Notice three small positive moments every day (e.g., someone smiled at you, you had a nice cup of tea, you completed a small task). Keep a gratitude diary.	
	Mindfulness Practice a mindful activity.	
	Nutrition Stay hydrated; eat healthy food.	
	Rest Get plenty of rest. Take a break.	
	Go Outdoors Get some fresh air, look at nature, look at the sky.	
	Exercise Take some exercise you enjoy – dancing, running, walking, yoga.	

Session 10 Course Review and Celebration

Facilitator Notes

Session Aims

The main purpose of this session is to help the students recognise that this is only the start of their path to a less anxious and more confident future. We wish to celebrate their attendance and the work done so far and to instil confidence that they can continue to improve.

We will remind the students of all the content covered in the course and encourage them to reflect on which parts have been, or may be, helpful for them. We will assist the students in creating an individualised action plan to take away and encourage them to support one another with helpful suggestions for moving forward.

Theory

A range of theories have been used in this course. The approach has been an evolutionary one: that anxiety has developed as a useful emotion to help us protect ourselves, but too much anxiety is unhelpful in today's world. Cognitive-behavioural approaches have been used, drawing attention to the links between mind and body, thoughts and feelings. Established schools of thought, including yoga and mindfulness, have been drawn upon to extract strategies and to give students an introduction to methods they may wish to follow up further. Anxiety has also been considered within the frame of a healthy lifestyle.

Learning Points

Whilst anxiety cannot and should not be eradicated from our lives, it can be managed. The course has covered a wide range of approaches, and they will not all appeal to every student. It is the individual student's responsibility to trial different strategies and pick out those that work for them.

Students will need an aide memoire to assist them in remembering strategies learnt on this course and to bring them to mind in times of stress. Managing anxiety is a lifelong process, and students should look to adapting their strategies and incorporating new ones as they grow emotionally and intellectually.

We can all support one another by listening to each other, complimenting progress, and sharing good ideas. Students may wish to stay in touch with some or all other course participants.

DOI:10.4324/9781003180364-10

Script

Resources

Have this book available for any details the students may ask about, such as websites and video clips.

Handouts

10.1   Action Plan
10.2   Evaluation
10.3   Certificates

You may wish to bring copies of Handout 9.2: Aide Memoire, in case students have forgotten

Pens and paper (one paper per student and facilitator)

Students to bring Personal Goals from Session 1, Mindfulness Questionnaire from Session 6, and Aide Memoire from Session 9.

If the facilitator chose to keep copies of the students' personal goals, these can be brought to this session in case any students have lost their copies.

Refreshments as agreed in Session 9.

Purpose and Resources Required	Plan
Introduction Welcome Session 10 Content Students to Bring Their Own: • Personal Goals (from Session 1) • Mindfulness Questionnaire (from Session 2) • Aide Memoire (from Session 9)	*Welcome to the last session of this course. You have all worked very hard and learnt a great deal. I will miss our sessions together when we finish. Of course, learning to manage our anxiety is not something we can ever "tick off" and say we have finished; it is a set of skills we continue working on all our lives. Today, as well as celebrating and having some fun, we will go through the ideas and strategies we have covered in the course to remind you of what they are so you can pick your own favourites to keep and practise.* *Last week, I gave you an Aide Memoire and asked you to look over the work we have completed over the ten sessions and identify which strategies and exercises have been useful for you. Who has their Aide Memoire with them? I have some spares here for any who forgot. It may help you later to complete your Action Plan. If you have your Personal Goals from Session 1 and your Mindfulness Questionnaire from Session 6, these may also help you reflect on how far you have come, what you have found useful so far, and what concepts and strategies you would like to keep, going forward.* *Today, I want us to start by looking back to where we were at the start of the course, when we filled in our Personal Goals. It may be that you have met some or all your goals, changed your goals, or not met them. What is important is how much you have learnt and how prepared you are for continuing to grow. Learning to manage our anxiety is a lifelong goal and doesn't stop today.* *Of course, you will not remember everything, and we have only touched on a lot of different approaches and strategies to combat anxiety. You might wish to follow some of them up individually after the course.* *By the end of the session, you will have completed your own brief Action Plan to help your feel more positive and less stressed.* *I will then ask you to complete a brief evaluation of the course, which will help me in running future courses, and then we can celebrate our achievements over the last ten sessions.*

Purpose and Resources Required	*Plan*
Activity Re-visit the goals we set in Session 1 Handout 1.3: Personal Goals Handout 6.1: Mindfulness Questionnaire	*Now it's time to look at the goals we set for ourselves in Session 1. Of course, everyone knew a lot less then, so we could easily have changed our goals during the course.* *Where do you think you have made progress? Which are the areas that you would like to develop further? You might also wish to refer to your Mindfulness Questionnaire to look at your progress.* Allow time for self-reflection. *Who would like to share an area of progress and perhaps a next step or area where they seem to be a bit stuck?* Allow one person to share. Give congratulations where due and ask others to give compliments. *It's impressive that you have taken some steps forward; I am proud of you. Would you like help where you are stuck?* If so, encourage others to offer suggestions. Repeat with other students.
Overview	*It would be totally unrealistic to expect that in a ten-session course, we would have solved all of everyone's problems with anxiety. What we have done is introduce you to a variety of ways of managing it. No one has had time to trial all these ideas thoroughly, though I hope that everyone has picked up a few tricks along the way. Everyone will need to keep up with the strategies they have found useful and continue to consider other things to help them.* *"Eureka moments" are times when something suddenly clicks into place for us – when we suddenly understand something or see a way through that we didn't see before. For instance, in one of these courses, one student suddenly realised that he was not going to get rid of anxiety from his life altogether but that he was effectively learning to manage it. Do any eureka moments come to mind for you?*
Activity Develop Action Plan 9.2 Aide Memoire Handout 10.1: Action Plan	*Next, I would like you to look again at the Aide Memoire of the strategies and methods that I gave you last week.* Provide Aides Memoire for any who have forgotten theirs. Provide Handout 10.1: Action Plan. *It is important that you capture the skills and strategies that you think can work for you on paper/phone so that when you are stressed and cannot think clearly, you have something to refer to. The Action Plan is a very brief, simple way of doing that.* *Look at your Aide Memoire and choose strategies for your Action Plan for the:* • *Short term: very stressed mode* • *Medium term: developing new skills* • *Long term: lifestyle and outlook shifts* *You might wish to keep a copy of this with you, maybe on your phone or on a card in your bag. Don't forget this is the beginning of a path, not the end of the road!*

Purpose and Resources Required	*Plan*
Evaluation Handout 10.2: Evaluation	*I would like you to fill in this evaluation form.* *It will help me in running this course again to know what went well and whether I need to change anything.* *Thank you!*
Conclusion Ask about ways forward for the students.	If there is the possibility of a follow-up session in four to six weeks, this can be planned now. *Would it be helpful to have a follow-up session to see how we are all getting on? If so, when would work? What else could help you make progress? Who else will be able to help you remember and try your new skills and strategies? Can you help each other?*
Celebration Compliments from students to each other (optional) Pens and paper (optional) Handout 10.3: Certificates (optional)	*Now we are all going to write our names on a separate piece of paper. We are going to sit in a circle and pass the papers around the circle. Each time we get a paper with someone's name on it, we will write a compliment to that person, something we admire or like about them, a time they have said something helpful or contributed well to the group. Then we will pass the paper along until we each get our own back and read some nice things about ourselves. We can take these compliments with us to read when we need a boost.* The facilitator may choose to be a part of the circle or not. After the exercise, allow time for each student to read their own compliments silently. *How did it feel to receive compliments? Was anyone surprised by what they read?* This is an opportunity for the facilitator to give each student publicly a personally chosen compliment about what the facilitator has admired about each individual, their strengths, or their input to the course. If certificates are being given, they can be given here. *Thanks, everyone, you have been a great team. Now let's celebrate together with cake/juice/biscuits. You really deserve it!*

10.1 Action Plan

Name   **Date**

Short term: In-the-moment strategies to calm me down when I am anxious:

1...

2...

3...

Medium term: Developing new skills for my well-being and resilience:

1...

2...

3...

Longer term: Changing my lifestyle and my outlook:

1...

2...

3...

10.2 Evaluation

Helping Teens and Young Adults with Anxiety: A Ten-Session Programme
Please rate on a scale of 1 to 10 how useful you found:

Session 1 Understanding Anxiety
1 ——— 2 ——— 3 ——— 4 ——— 5 ——— 6 ——— 7 ——— 8 ——— 9 ——— 10

Session 2 Helpful and Unhelpful Coping Strategies
1 ——— 2 ——— 3 ——— 4 ——— 5 ——— 6 ——— 7 ——— 8 ——— 9 ——— 10

Session 3 How Anxiety Makes Our Bodies Feel
1 ——— 2 ——— 3 ——— 4 ——— 5 ——— 6 ——— 7 ——— 8 ——— 9 ——— 10

Session 4 Recognising, Understanding, and Managing Our Emotions
1 ——— 2 ——— 3 ——— 4 ——— 5 ——— 6 ——— 7 ——— 8 ——— 9 ——— 10

Session 5 Changing Our Thoughts
1 ——— 2 ——— 3 ——— 4 ——— 5 ——— 6 ——— 7 ——— 8 ——— 9 ——— 10

Session 6 Mindfulness
1 ——— 2 ——— 3 ——— 4 ——— 5 ——— 6 ——— 7 ——— 8 ——— 9 ——— 10

Session 7 Facing Our Fears
1 ——— 2 ——— 3 ——— 4 ——— 5 ——— 6 ——— 7——— 8 ——— 9 ——— 10

Session 8 Lifestyle
1 ——— 2 ——— 3 ——— 4 ——— 5 ——— 6 ——— 7 ——— 8 ——— 9 ——— 10

Session 9 Identifying Our Strengths
1 ——— 2 ——— 3 ——— 4 ——— 5 ——— 6 ——— 7 ——— 8 ——— 9 ——— 10

Session 10 The Course Review and Celebration

1 ——— 2 ——— 3 ——— 4 ——— 5 ——— 6 ——— 7 ——— 8 ——— 9 ——— 10

The course as a whole

1 ——— 2 ——— 3 ——— 4 ——— 5 ——— 6 ——— 7 ——— 8 ——— 9 ——— 10

How likely would you be to recommend this course to others?

1 ——— 2 ——— 3 ——— 4 ——— 5 ——— 6 ——— 7 ——— 8 ——— 9 ——— 10

What was the part you liked least?

What was the part you liked best?

Any other comments?

SUPPORT MATERIAL 10.3 Certificate for Teens/Young Adults

CERTIFICATE OF ATTENDANCE

This Certificate is awarded to

_____

for attendance at

_____

on

_____

_____
Signature

_____
Date

Index

Note: **Boldfaced** page references indicate tables. *Italic* references indicate worksheets.

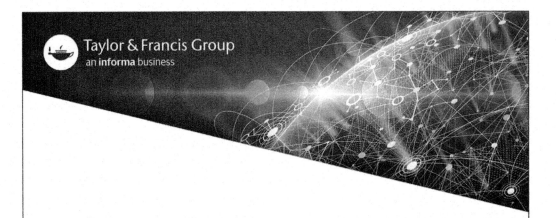